SPARK

CREATIVE INSPIRATION
ANTHOLOGY

2019 EDITION

PRESENTED BY ⬡ SHOWIT

SHOWIT

Visit our website at showit.co.

Copywriting: Cassandra Campbell, Jihae Watson,
Sarah Kay Love, Jasmine Star, Davey & Krista Jones,
Ashlyn Carter, Andra Barkey, Kelly Zugay,
Jeff Willems

Cover photo: David Mendoza III

Design: Jed Smith, Nate Sees

ISBN 978-0-692-19935-0

Printed in China

A single spark nestled in a bed of dry kindling has the power to ignite into flame, flooding the wooden tipi around it with light, illuminating the cold, dark night with life and warmth. However, the spark alone doesn't guarantee the fire. It takes the right mixture of fuel and oxygen to take a spark and grow it into a vibrant, thriving fire.

What an exquisite parallel to one's own creative journey. Do you remember your spark? That idea that began as a dream in your mind, which then caught fire in your heart, burning passion as it's fuel, fanned by the love and support of others around you? That one little spark changed your life, and it is why you do what you do today. Maybe you haven't found that spark yet, and you're hoping this book can help.

We believe it can.

We believe in the overwhelming power of community. So much so, in fact, that we printed 50 of the most awe-inspiring websites we could find in this book. We could have sent you the link to each of those sites, but that would miss the point. Inspiration, as much as creation, is a process. Different mediums, genres, moments, and people inspire us all along the way in our journeys. We wanted to create something different, an inspiration for your online presence that you could hold in your hands, make notes right on the page, or take on a weekend vision planning retreat at a little cabin in the woods with no wifi.

We hope you find enjoyment and inspiration in the following pages. So grab a cup of coffee, curl up in a comfortable spot, and dive in. Admire the artistry of your creative peers, and appreciate the beauty of their fire, burning bright for all to see in these pages, which all started from one small spark of creativity, fueled by passion, and fanned by an encouraging and uplifting community.

TODD WATSON
SHOWIT CO-FOUNDER / CEO

TABLE OF CONTENTS

MODERNE REVERIE

🌐 MODERNEREVERIE.COM

In 2009, Lindsey Shaun Christensen and Kenzie Victory combined their vast experiences in the wedding industry to create a perfectly curated site committed to celebrating "the organic nature of two people in love." With an image-heavy blog, they forfeited traditional format in favor of a website devoted to bridal inspiration with an emphasis on visual navigation. Lindsey, the co-owner and designer of the site, applies her keen eye in the sifting of hundreds of images from a wedding, to finding the perfect cover photo to entice her visitors to click through the blog post. ModerneReverie.com is sure to be any future bride's favorite site to spark ideas for her pending nuptials, as well as elevate the featured photographers and connect vendors with new clients.

DESIGNED FROM SCRATCH
IN SHOWIT

COLORS

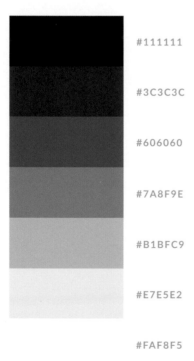

#111111

#3C3C3C

#606060

#7A8F9E

#B1BFC9

#E7E5E2

#FAF8F5

#FFFFFF

TYPEFACES

Quattrocento Sans

EB Garamond Normal

EB Garamond Italic

Garamond

WELCOME TO MODERNE REVERIE

INSPIRING BRIDES SINCE 2009

moderne reverie

FORMERLY UTAH BRIDE BLOG

WELCOME TO MODERNE REVERIE

INSPIRING BRIDES SINCE 2009

DREAM SUMMER WEDDING

DREAM SUMMER WEDDING

ALBION BASIN MAGIC

A note from the editors:

WE ARE LOOKING FOR IMAGES OF THE FOLLOWING TO FEATURE IN OUR MONTHLY TRENDS WE LOVE.

UNIQUE CAKES

OUT OF STATE WEDDING, SHOT BY A UTAH PHOTOGRAPHER

HONEYMOON LOCATION FAVS

CURRENT COLOR FAVORITES:

TRENDS WE'RE LOVING

SNAKE RIVER FORMALS

mariko kay

Flora & Flourish

RYAN HINMAN
- FILMS -

STUDIO B&W ENGAGEMENTS

NYC INSPIRED WEDDING

blushing rose floral

Sleepy Ridge
WEDDINGS

MANDI RAE

FELICIA THE PHOTOGRAPHER

🌐 FELICIATHEPHOTOGRAPHER.COM

It's a simple start, but clever as anything. From the first moment on her website, Felicia Ramirez keeps your attention because of her proposal to work together. The details? Subtle shifts in light and dark, close-up and distant, color and black and white. These details are her initial slideshow that showcases her work. While most photographers will keep their highlight reel relegated to one congruent style, Felicia does the opposite, and it creates a very memorable journey through her site. Even her portfolio page stands out with the contrast of different weddings selected for the visitor to enjoy. This custom site by the photographer herself is bold, intentional, and a stand-out that Felicia should feel so very proud of!

DESIGNED FROM SCRATCH
IN SHOWIT

COLORS

#1C1C1C

#282828

#847D6A

#CCC0A0

#ECEBE8

#FFFFFF

TYPEFACES

Oswald Light

Oswald

CINZEL NORMAL

Roman Serif

Honeyscript Light

HOME   FELICIA   PORTFOLIO   INFORMATION   INQUIRE   BLOG

well, hello there!

I photograph gorgeous weddings for bold, adventurous, and crazy-in-love couples all over this beautiful earth! I love getting to know my clients on a personal level, and to me, the privilege of capturing the most special day of their lives is a dream. Take a look around at some of the love stories I've been delighted to eternalize!

xoxo felicia

ENGAGEMENTS   WEDDINGS   PORTRAITS

WHAT BRIDES ARE SAYING

KRISSY + RYAN   ANDREA + SASHA   VANESSA + ZACH

"Felicia is just an absolute dream-   "Felicia is a DREAM. From start to   "Words cannot describe how happy

ASHLEY TRACY PHOTOGRAPHY

🌐 ASHLEYTRACYPHOTOGRAPHY.COM

It's unclear if her tagline came first or if it was the moments she kept capturing that stuck out. It is clear however, that Ashley Tracy has found her ideal client. When it came time to put it into a web design, Sarah Crook of Alisabeth Designs, was enlisted to express Ashley's desire to capture "chasing sunsets, scrunchy-nosed laughter, and joyful closeness!" The powerful shots of couples doing just this are splashed across the screen from the first click to the final scroll of AshleyTracyPhotography.com. All along the way, her natural light photography is center stage, with hand-drawn details, and simple chalked squares to frame the image and entice the brides to see more. With well-established brand presence, more couples will be hoping to get in front of Ashley's camera to "go from passionate kisses to tickle-fests in five seconds or less."

DESIGNED BY

SARAH CROOK
ALISABETH DESIGNS

ALISABETHDESIGNS.COM

COLORS

#000000

#21150C

#442214

#9B622D

#E7CEAD

#F7F1E8

#F3F2EC

#FFFFFF

TYPEFACES

PT Serif Normal

Wild Spirit

Josefin Sans Normal

Josefin Sans Light

Ashley Tracy
PHOTOGRAPHY

sunsets, scrunchy-nosed

Ashley Tracy
PHOTOGRAPHY

sunsets, scrunchy-nosed laughter, and joyful closeness

Hey there,
I'M ASHLEY

A Natural Light Photographer, based in Barnesville, Ohio - doin' life with my handsome hubs and beautiful little girl. Chasing light with clients who love deeply, laugh loudly, and aren't afraid of a little photo session acrobatics are some of my favorite things to do. And when I'm not working I'm either running around, with my family - or binge watching The Office for the 100th time, on Netflix.
(Bears ... Beets ... Battlestar Galactica!)

HERE'S WHAT SETS MY SOUL ON FIRE ...

Raves & REVIEWS

OOH, I WANNA READ MORE!

RAELENE SCHULMEISTER PHOTOGRAPHY

🌐 RAELENESCHULMEISTER.COM

With a rainbow-hued "Raelene" greeting each visitor, a sense of fun has taken priority over all else. But, as brides-to-be follow the colorful borders, they quickly learn that Raelene Schulmeister Photography has the skill to match all the bright sparkles. Raelene's provincial images of couples cuddling at sunset or strolling along Canadian fields is juxtaposed from her almost tropical branding. When working with Ally B Designs, Raelene told her: "My brand is full of bright colours that pop, a little bit sassy and just 100% me!" Even the free download on her site, *The Beginner's Checklist to Planning Your Wedding with Humor*, assures her visitors she can help make their day a happy one! Brides will ecstatically be downloading while simultaneously scrolling for the contact prompt, with a huge smile on their face!

DESIGNED BY

ALICIA BAUER
ALLY B DESIGNS

ALLYBDESIGNS.COM

COLORS

#B0AAAA

#77D7C9

#F03F97

#E0F352

#666666

#BFBFBF

#ECEBE8

#FFFFFF

TYPEFACES

Montserrat Light

Open Sans Light

Playfair Display Italic

Bordeaux

Raelene
SCHULMEISTER
PHOTOGRAPHY

GET PHOTOS THAT MAKE YOU *Happy*

AND A PHOTOGRAPHER YOU'RE EXCITED TO WORK WITH

Raelene
SCHULMEISTER
PHOTOGRAPHY

Do you...

WANT PHOTOS SO GOOD THEY'LL HAVE YOU RELIVING YOUR WEDDING DAY OVER AND OVER?

WHAT ABOUT A PHOTOGRAPHER WHO KNOWS HOW TO DO MORE THAN JUST SNAP MOMENTS AS THEY HAPPEN?

YOUR WEDDING'S GONNA BE SO MUCH FUN AND YOU'RE GONNA LOOK AMAZING.

let's create images that tell your story and show how it all went down

CHECK OUT MY WEDDING PHOTOGRAPHY AND ENGAGEMENT PACKAGES

GET PHOTOS THAT

IF YOU VALUE LASTING PHOTOS WORTHY OF DISPLAY THROUGHOUT YOUR HOME

(NOT JUST ON INSTA OR FACEBOOK)

FLIP THROUGH MY ONLINE PORTFOLIO

love notes

Thank you, thank you, thank you again for the incredible pictures, the amazing memories OFF camera, and all of the support and humour you brought to our day!

SAM + ANDY

want to see more! ▶

SHOW ME MORE OF YOUR WORK!

AMY MURGATROYD PORTRAITS + FILMS

🌐 AMYMURGATROYD.COM

As sweet scenes of families run across the screen when you first enter Amy's site, visitors are met with delight and awe in each image. Shortly following, "Amy Murgatroyd Portraits + Films" is hand-lettered across the screen as if happening in real time. And the whimsical attention to detail doesn't end there! The charming arboreal illustrations whisk you through the site and Amy's joy-filled captures. As each life-giving family or portrait photo crosses the screen, the visitor will find themselves automatically slowing their scroll as to not miss anything. And when they head to the "About" page to learn more about the photographer behind these intimate family portraits, they will find out the reason designer Louise Ross, of The Autumn Rabbit, has incorporated it into the site. And, if it were even possible, Amy's visitor will feel even more compelled to work with her.

DESIGNED BY

LOUISE ROSS
THE AUTUMN RABBIT

THEAUTUMNRABBIT.COM

COLORS

#1A0A10

#30131E

#4D1E30

#DED7CD

#F9F7F5

#9DAA98

#849BA0

#FFFFFF

TYPEFACES

Rosarivo Normal

Rosarivo Italic

Lato Normal

Lato Italic

Lato Light

Lato Light Italic

14

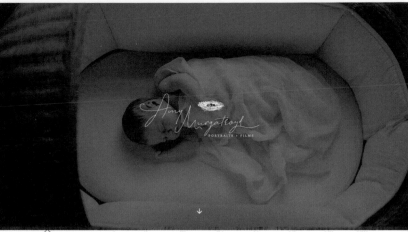

ABOUT *amy* · *portrait* SESSIONS · DOCUMENTARY *sessions* · *family* FILMS · RECENT *sessions* · *for* PHOTOGS · THE *details* · *contact* ME

PORTRAITS & FAMILY FILMS

unscripted
EMOTIVE
sincere

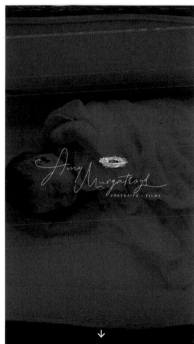

welcome

your moments matter because your people do.

We're not going for "the shot" and we won't try for something you're not. I want your connection not your perfection. My role isn't to create beauty but to receive yours as a family and translate it into images that mirror your heart for each other.

LEAH FONTAINE PHOTOGRAPHY

🌐 LEAHFONTAINE.COM

In a profession driven by visuals, it's important to make your first impression big and bold. From playful script to the lively faces of newlyweds, Leah Fontaine's statement to her potential clients is, "joy lives here and I'm excited you've found it." This quote is splashed across the page immediately after you have found her big and bold choices of images overtaking the computer screen of elated couples. Describing her own photographic style as "vibrant, joyful, and genuine," one might add "daring". Not in a rebellious manner, but as she states on her website, one of her goals is to make everyone feel "much cooler than me." The carefully chosen fonts match Leah's fun and loving personality, compliment her stunning photos, and highlight her clever words that will surely have any bride-to be wanting Leah by her side on her big day.

DESIGNED BY

LOUISE ROSS
THE AUTUMN RABBIT

THEAUTUMNRABBIT.COM

COLORS

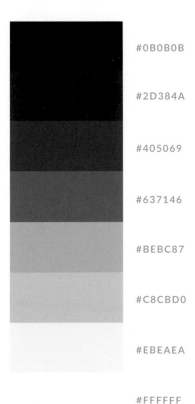

#0B0B0B

#2D384A

#405069

#637146

#BEBC87

#C8CBD0

#EBEAEA

#FFFFFF

TYPEFACES

Montserrat

Lato Normal

Fjalla One

Madina

LEAH
fontaine
PHOTOGRAPHY

joy LIVES HERE
and I'm excited you've found it!

Hey you guys! I'm Leah, a Minnesota based wedding + family photographer, passionate about living life out loud!

I'm into happy tears, laughing until your cheeks hurt, and running because you feel like you could burst from excitement! I'm heavy handed on encouraging the joy and excitement of your wedding day, allowing your photos to live and breathe, preserving your happiness of your epic day for a lifetime.

LEAH
fontaine
PHOTOGRAPHY

DOES YOUR WEDDING DAY INCLUDE RUNNING HAND IN HAND TOWARDS THE SUN?

⊗ YES!

◯ NO! *(you want to check yes, I promise!)*

WEDDING
experience

GALLERIES

view
THE BLOG

SCHRAGE PHOTOGRAPHY

🌐 SCHRAGEPHOTOGRAPHY.COM

The goal of any website is to entice the visitor to stay and look around in the matter of mere seconds. Leigh Schrage, of SchragePhotography.com, has surmounted the obstacle with a split screen of her perfectly lit images, brilliantly balanced font pairings, and focused message. The sweet mid-western images on her site are matched with words to evoke emotion not common to a wedding and portrait photographer. But that's because Leigh is not just any common photographer. Leigh catches her ideal client's attention by being herself. Unabashedly, totally, and completely herself. The visitors will arrive and stay because of her beautiful images displayed with watercolor backgrounds and eye-catching parallax, using the Freya design by The Autumn Rabbit. But, they will press "Contact Me" because Leigh has found a way to set herself apart, by sharing the thoughts that her ideal client will be sure to relate to.

DESIGNED WITH
FREYA BY THE AUTUMN RABBIT

COLORS

#101D26

#344538

#617764

#EFF0F1

#5C2931

#E1D1C4

#F2F2ED

#FFFFFF

TYPEFACES

Cormorant Garamond Normal

Cormorant Garamond Italic

Pinyon Script Normal

Lanara

For the *romantic* couple,
madly *in love...*

hello
love

I AM SO GLAD THAT
YOU DROPPED BY!!

I'm Leigh, a wedding and portrait
photographer in the land of 10,000
lakes. I'm a lover of light, true
love and everything authentic.

Want to know more?

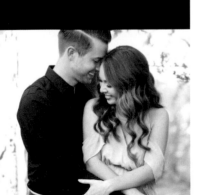

For the *romantic* couple,
madly *in love...*

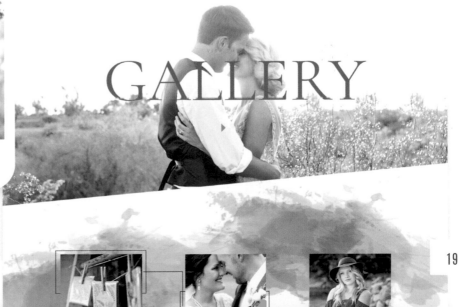

GALLERY

PURE IN ART PHOTOGRAPHY

🌐 PUREINART.COM

With a clear and detailed vision of who her dream client is, Tina Marie Kraemer, the photographer and owner of Pure in Art Photography, has an online home that perfectly reflects her brand. With the help of designer Amanda Csakan of Brand Epiphany, PureInArt.com marries fresh and modern with traditional and warm. Choosing a soft color palette, Tina's airy and romantic photography is perfectly complemented with her brand colors of blush and copper. An excellent addition to Tina's site is the detailed timeline of "The Process," so brides can know exactly what to expect when booking. Tina is so thankful that her new brand and website are finally reflecting her heart and passion. Not only that, but her online home is attracting clients who are looking for a touch of pure art on their special day.

DESIGNED BY

AMANDA CSAKAN
BRAND EPIPHANY

BRANDEPIPHANY.COM

COLORS

#394D63

#6D6E70

#869AAE

#C6B578

#E5C3B9

#F6F6F6

#F7F7F5

#FFFFFF

TYPEFACES

Questrial Normal

Cardo Normal

Cardo Bold

Cardo Italic

MENU

EST. 2011

PURE IN ART
PHOTOGRAPHY

view the
PORTFOLIO

meet
TINA

the experience
FOR BRIDES

read past couples'
LOVE NOTES

read the
BLOG

get in
CONTACT

Photography for joyful couples who crave a stress-free celebration of their wedding day and desire candid images that reflect their love.

MENU ⌄

EST. 2011

PURE IN ART
PHOTOGRAPHY

Photography for joyful couples who crave a stress-free celebration of their wedding day and desire candid images that reflect their love.

MEET TINA

A midwestern girl who fell in love with the romance of the desert. I love ice cream, cooking for my friends and loving people well.

LEARN MORE

THE EXPERIENCE

Joyfully celebrating your relationship, our time together is a thoughtful preservation of your most treasured moments.

LEARN MORE

EDUCATION

As an educator with a background in photography and graphic design, I believe the key to growth is leading and learning from others. I offer workshops and mentoring as a means to encourage community.

LEARN MORE

AS SEEN ON

LAUREN BUMAN PHOTOGRAPHY

 LAURENBUMAN.COM

What's pretty in pink, and fun yet refined? LaurenBuman.com, that's what! Amanda Csakan of Brand Epiphany, was able to take Lauren's three descriptive words for her brand: "Modern, Sophisticated, Feminine", and bring them to life. And Lauren could not be more thrilled. The second her homepage is displayed, a lively image of a bride and groom with pink balloons greets you and leaves a lasting impression as you scroll through the rest of this sweet site. You can tell she is a talented photographer from the work exhibited, but you can also tell from her "Meet Lauren" section that she is going to be a great fit at your pretty and joyous wedding. She will be your "sixth bridesmaid", and probably a true friend even after your wedding, which is why she refers to her website visitors as "Frient: friend + client"! See? So fun!

DESIGNED BY

AMANDA CSAKAN
BRAND EPIPHANY

BRANDEPIPHANY.COM

COLORS

#253E38

#F4CDA4

#5E5E5E

#FEC9BF

#294360

#FFF9F8

#F5F5F5

#FFFFFF

TYPEFACES

Old Standard TT Normal

Old Standard TT Italic

Anter

Oswald Light

Lato Normal

LAUREN BUMAN
PHOTOGRAPHY

modern, joyful, feminine

oh hey, hi!

I'm Lauren and I visually tell love stories here in Arizona.

From our first meeting, over coffee (or cocktails) I want to hear how it all began, I want to know all about the day something shiny was slipped on your hand, and I absolutely want to know where y'all ate!

I can typically be found in the kitchen, either frying a piece of chicken, willing a picky toddler to eat her veggies, or making a giant french press, for one, please!

I believe in »

modern, joyful, feminine

GALLERIES

01. blush garden wedding
02. colorful garden wedding
03. scottsdale blush wedding
04. engagement gallery
05. portrait gallery

MORE ABOUT THE EXPERIENCE

RAVES

Lauren was friendly, kind, and very

BUILDING
A BRAND

with JASMINE STAR

What is the first thing you suggest to creatives when they start to build their website and want to successfully incorporate their brand?

The key to all marketing is simple...you know exactly who you're selling to. You need to have a crystal clear picture of who that person is, what s/he wants, what s/he desires, what makes them excited when they find your website. When I create my Ideal Client Profile, I also include small details about where they shop, what magazines they read, their most recent YouTube search, where they last went on vacation, and a litany of other details. In order for me to create a standout website, I need to know who, precisely, I'm selling to and make it perfect for him/her.

How can a branded website enhance your marketing goals or increase revenue?

Listen, it's easy to look at other competitors in your field and begin stacking up reasons your business is unique, but if you cannot show that visually, prospective customers won't be able to tell. For all intents and purposes, a photographer is a photographer is a photographer. How do you stick out in a saturated market? Create a website that is totally reflective of YOU and the people you want to work with.

Are there any mistakes you see creatives do when building website that fits their brand?

I can't speak of mistakes, per se, but I can tell you that when I visit a website of a professional who does 127 things at once, I immediately close the browser. In today's day and age, it's easy to think that we must do everything and be everyone. I'm a strong believer in specializing and creating a niche before I attempt to showcase a mix of businesses on one website.

Can you give some advice on how professionals can remain true to themselves, their brand and business when building their website?

Work with a graphic designer you trust. Often times creatives (you and me both) get caught up in our heads. We over-analyze, we overthink, we get overwhelmed. When you work with someone else, they simply hold up a mirror to what you want and help guide the truest conversations about your objectives...then set a clear strategy to get it done.

Are there specific features you love about the Showit platform that can help creatives accomplish a beautiful branded website?

Great Question! I don't know if it's a "feature", but can we just talk about the Showit support team?! I've worked with other platforms before and it'd take DAYS or WEEKS before I'd get a response to my tech questions. The Showit team goes above and beyond to ensure my website is exactly what I want and need. They're the true super heroes. With a team like that, the features are important...but they are worth more when you have a group of supporters pushing you forward!

EPIC EVENT PLANNING

🌐 EPICEVENTPLANNING.NET

Shericca Bittle is the creative genius with the huge heart behind Epic Event Planning. She teamed up with Bernel from Branded by Bernel to create a luxurious, modern, interactive, and EPIC website! Along with the gorgeous images from events she has planned, Shericca shares the personal story behind her business. It all started with her own wedding, sadly having no wedding pictures, and no "dress of her dreams" from her own wedding, simply because it was all so overwhelming. This is the "why" of her business. Shericca truly creates unforgettable events through tiny details, and this is how her website was built as well. "Most of my clients that find me on social media tell me that after they viewed my website, that was what sold them." With a clear message, and a great designer, Epic Event Planning will ensure no bride has to miss out on any detail of her wedding with Shericca by her side.

DESIGNED BY

BERNEL WESTBROOK
BRANDED BY BERNEL

BRANDEDBYBERNEL.COM

COLORS

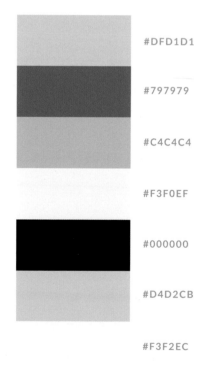

#DFD1D1

#797979

#C4C4C4

#F3F0EF

#000000

#D4D2CB

#F3F2EC

#FFFFFF

TYPEFACES

Raleway Normal

Libre Baskerville Normal

Didot

Lora

Nometica

26

WELCOME

WE TRANSFORM SMALL DETAILS INTO

epic events

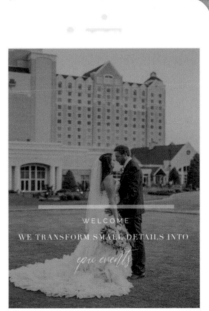

epic
EVENT PLANNING

HOME   ABOUT SHERICCA   SERVICES   LOOKBOOK   BLOG   CONTACT US

CONGRATULATIONS ON YOUR *epic* / MILESTONE

Epic Event Planning is a full service wedding and event planning company based in Greensboro, North Carolina. we service any of the surrounding cities and beyond. We are detailed-oriented, organized, creative and are Certified Wedding Planners through the Association of Bridal Consultants. Our mission is to make the happiest day of your life beautiful and stress free

MEET SHERICCA

A COMPLETLEY UNIQUE

WEDDING EXPERIENCE

If you are the couple that has big beautiful dreams for your wedding day, but much rather spend the time enjoying your engagement rather than stressing out. Then you have come to the right place! Take a deep breath, we are here to transform your small details into an EPIC event.

LEARN MORE

WELCOME

WE TRANSFORM SMALL DETAILS INTO

epic events

epic
EVENT PLANNING

CONGRATULATIONS ON YOUR

FEATURED IN

 Home Confetti   MunaLuchi Bride   BLACK SOUTHERN BELLE   FEATURED WEDDING VENDOR   Borrowed & Blue WEDDINGS | Marry Me

READ SOME OF OUR

LOVE NOTES

‹ Thank you for a wonderful wedding!! As MOB, I could not have asked for a better wedding planner! Your talent really shinned through on the ideals that you had. What a beautiful ceremony & reception it was!! Everyone was saying how beautiful everything turned out to be!! I want to say thank you for the beautiful wedding Amanda had, and all the countless hours that you put into it to make her day was special. ›

Patrice

EPIC EVENT PLANNING

WE TRANSFORM THE SMALL
DETAILS INTO EPIC EVENTS

LET'S PLAN YOUR NEXT EVENT

BASED IN GREENSBORO NC, SERVING THE TRIAD

EPICEVENTPLANNINGINFO@GMAIL.COM

© 2018 EPIC EVENT PLANNING

WEB DESIGN
BY BRANDED BY
BERNEL

THE PRETTY DETAILS

@EPIC_EVENT_PLANNING

27

ABBY ANDERSON

🌐 ABBYANDERSON.COM

Photographer Abby Anderson and designer Christina Laing of The Buffalo Collective, worked together to create a completely custom and unique website. Brides-to-be will be smitten by everything on AbbyAnderson.com, from the absolutely lovely logo, to Abby's vibrant and romantic images. Further along the site, they will notice colorful brand accents of gold and deep purple to give an air of royalty without being stuffy and pretentious, but instead, chic and elegant. Abby has been quite happy with the new look, and her visitors turned clients agree! "After launching this site, my photographic voice was strengthened and my business grew tremendously. It provided a high-end frame for the images and trademarked my style in an increasingly saturated market. In a recent survey, brides pointed to this website as the place where they spent the most time researching my work." That is exactly what a great website is supposed to do!

DESIGNED BY

CHRISTINA LAING
THE BUFFALO COLLECTIVE

THEBUFFALOCOLLECTIVE.COM

COLORS

#2D2D2D

#284844

#A62561

#F8DADB

#EAC487

#FFFFFF

TYPEFACES

Antic Didone Normal

Old Standard TT Italic

Montserrat

Lora

Playfair Display Italic

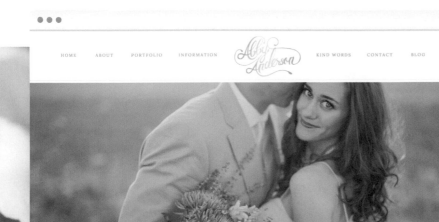

HOME   ABOUT   PORTFOLIO   INFORMATION   *Abby Anderson*   KIND WORDS   CONTACT   BLOG   SENIOR GIRLS

HELLO *and* WELCOME

Vibrant Lovestories, Modern Fairytales

MEET ABBY

Hello! I'm Abby Anderson, a Midwestern girl with a passion for dramatic flair and happy endings. My photography is driven by a fascination with light and finding beauty wherever I go. My family, friends and relationship with Jesus inspire me every day. When I'm not behind the camera, you're likely to find me drinking tea or cooking something delicious in my kitchen. I live in Moorhead, MN with my husband and two daughters.

MY PHILOSOPHY ▸

HELLO *and* WELCOME
Vibrant Lovestories, Modern Fairytales

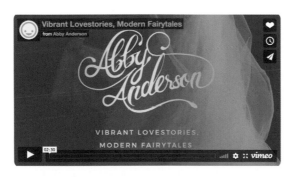

Vibrant Lovestories, Modern Fairytales
from Abby Anderson

Abby Anderson

VIBRANT LOVESTORIES,
MODERN FAIRYTALES

02:30   vimeo

BRIGHT EYED *and* FULL OF LIFE,
she grew up with the wind in her hair, running barefoot
and swimming weekends away at the lake.

ATHENA & CAMRON

🌐 ATHENAANDCAMRON.COM

Athena and Camron are lovers of the unposed and intimate. They capture every image this way, and find great joy in teaching others their technique. Upon opening AthenaandCamron.com, visitors will be able to guess the couple's location (the Pacific Northwest) and their ideal client (unposed and intimate). "Our most received compliment since our launch earlier this year has been how our website feels in every way like an invitation to a great and beautiful story." The couple's online home is a breath of cool, fresh air! Using the *Harlow* template by The Buffalo Collective, Athena and Camron have built a custom online home that perfectly reflects them: "clean, minimal, straight edge design collided with earthy tones, fun images and the written word." Together, the couple has designed every element of their site to show who they are, prioritizing intuitive and easy to use design, giving visitors the chance see true connection in action.

DESIGNED WITH
HARLOW BY THE BUFFALO COLLECTIVE

COLORS

#242424

#545454

#5F6574

#B5BAC3

#9A7E5F

#B29D84

#E7E7E7

#FFFFFF

TYPEFACES

Shopping Script

Brandon Grotesque

Oswald Light

ATHENA & CAMRON

ABOUT

We are husband + wife, and think marriage is the best thing ever.

Based in the Pacific North West, we are wedding photographers and educators of the unposed and intimate.

If your marriage matters to you even more than your wedding day, then we're your photographers!

ATHENA & CAMRON

LATEST BLOG POSTS

VIEW

WANT A FREE PRESET?

HECK YES

PEPPERMINT TEA PHOTOGRAPHY

Pamela Jacobsen of Peppermint Tea Photography needed a website to spotlight the concierge experience she offers her clients. Using the *Ellicott* design by The Buffalo Collective, she found the perfect jumping-off point to create an informative and gracefully-refined website. "I receive more inquiries because visitors have a clearer understanding of the experience I offer." While Pamela has customized her online storefront to "focus on a luxury experience that is personal," she has also added special touches that allow each visitor to relate to her as an individual as well as a photographer. One section that draws potential clients in is the "Giving Back" portion where Pamela talks about photographing families in the NICU. Sharing her heart for her clients and desire to give back really sets PeppermintTeaPhotography.com apart.

DESIGNED WITH
ELLICOTT BY THE BUFFALO COLLECTIVE

COLORS

#000000

#3E3E3E

#616161

#7C7C7C

#AEAEAE

#C9C9C9

#F5F5F5

#FFFFFF

TYPEFACES

Cormorant Garamond Normal

Aire Roman Pro

Brandon Grotesque

Mrs Saint Delafield Normal

WELCOME

THE LOVE FOR WHAT WE DO STARTS WITH YOU

With each breath, time continues to pass and we need to be present by stamping each moment with everything our hearts stand for. Through photography, we have the opportunity to forever hold a piece of your legacy, today, tomorrow and in 20 years as your family grows. The greatest gift you can give someone you love is a piece of this legacy and through photos it is possible. Make time stand still so YOUR stories of today will have a voice tomorrow.

YOUR LEGACY

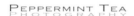

WELCOME

THE LOVE FOR WHAT WE DO STARTS WITH YOU

With each breath, time continues to pass and we need to be present by stamping each moment with everything our hearts stand for. Through photography, we have the opportunity to forever hold a piece of your legacy, today, tomorrow and in 20

YOUR STORY

DOCUMENTING THOSE IN BETWEEN MOMENTS

With my lifestyle artistic approach, I simply document your unscripted moments, the moments in between, because those are the ones filled with *real life*. Whether it is the smile brought on by those sweet whispers, the inside chatter that made you laugh, or the beauty that made you cry...these are stories you will want to relive again and again.

"YOU CAN'T GET TIME BACK
WITH SOMEONE
BUT YOU CAN RELIVE
IT THROUGH A PHOTOGRAPH."
Click To Read The Story Behind
Peppermint Tea Photography

HANNAH BLACK PHOTOGRAPHY

🌐 HANNAHBLACKPHOTOGRAPHY.COM

It would be tempting for any designer to take Hannah's last name and use it as a jumping off point when creating a website. But Amanda of Carrylove Designs took this photographer's "colorful, vibrant, joy-filled" brand and put it on a pedestal. With bursts of nearly neon, Hannah's images pop out against vertical black and white stripes, further emphasizing her energetic style. Directing brides and seniors to opposite directions with a punchy script and illustrated poppy pink and pale green arrows, all clients will feel well-served with their separate and engaging galleries. And getting to know Hannah is just as fun. Her "About" section stands out with unique icons and she describes what those images mean to her—and to her clients. Having thought through each design element to draw in web visitors, Amanda and Hannah have combined their artistic powers to create one super site.

DESIGNED BY

AMANDA SHUMAN
CARRYLOVE DESIGNS

CARRYLOVEDESIGNS.COM

COLORS

#F5DD09

#AFDED6

#E61D6B

#F1B2C5

#EBEBEB

#000000

#FFFFFF

TYPEFACES

Montserrat Bold

Montserrat Normal

Montserrat Light

Silver South Script

SILVER SOUTH SERIF

Hannah Black
PHOTOGRAPHY

ABOUT
SENIORS
BRIDES
BLOG
CONTACT

Hannah Black Photography specializes in Seniors and Wedding Photography. Based in Austin, Texas with a great love for adventure.

VIBRANT, JOYFUL, GENUINE

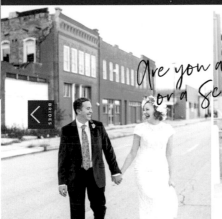

Are you a Bride or a Senior?

BRIDES

SENIORS

hannah black

MEET HANNAH

NICE TO MEET YOU!

I'm a small town Texas girl that's in love with living near Austin. I'm married to my high school sweetheart. You can find me waking up before the sun, drinking iced soy chai, and taking care of all my plants. Laughing is my literal favorite thing.

the full story »

INSTAGRAM IS MY JAM

LET'S CONNECT
@hannahblackphoto

ABOUT

Hannah Black Photography specializes in Seniors and Wedding Photography. Based in Austin, Texas with a great love for adventure.

Hannah Black
PHOTOGRAPHY

LIKE WHAT YOU SEE?

LET'S WORK TOGETHER!

LET'S GET SOCIAL

© 2018 Hannah Black Photography | Brand + Site Design by Carrylove Designs

MENU

Hannah Black
PHOTOGRAPHY

VIBRANT, JOYFUL, GENUINE

Hannah Black Photography specializes in Seniors and Wedding Photography. Based in Austin, Texas with a great love for adventure.

ELIZABETH HENSON PHOTOS INC

🌐 ELIZABETHHENSONPHOTOS.COM

Sharing unique aspects of yourself might be the thing that helps you to really connect with your ideal client. In Elizabeth Henson's case, that meant crafting a brand that resonates with "couples who love heirlooms, happy hour, and questionable dance moves." With a soft color palette, her images of those heirlooms are mingled in galleries and slideshows with smiling, over-joyed couples and their crew. A simple, yet distinct scripted font gives visitors the impression that Elizabeth has personally composed this greeting. Starting off with a design template by Go Live, and having Amanda of CarryLove Designs customize it, ElizabethHensonPhotos.com is the perfectly lovely and organic online home that Elizabeth needs. As an educator, podcaster, as well as a fantastic photographer, everyone will find Elizabeth, and every facet of her businesses, inviting and engaging.

CUSTOMIZED BY

AMANDA SHUMAN
CARRYLOVE DESIGNS

CARRYLOVEDESIGNS.COM

COLORS

#343434

#7E7E7E

#759B5B

#FDE4D1

#F7E05E

#C3C3C3

#F2F2F2

#FFFFFF

TYPEFACES

Oswald Light

TRASHHAND

Playfair Display Normal

Playfair Display Italic

Raleway Light

WEDDINGS   ABOUT Elizabeth   INFORMATION

BLOG   EDUCATION FOR Creatives   CONTACT

Where couples dance to their own beat and heirlooms never go out of style . . .

WELCOME

MEET ELIZABETH

A creative dreamer and over achiever...

Most days you can find me at my computer jamming out to some 90s music. I love my job. I mean I REALLY love it. My clients trust my humor and they feel my passion for my work. I'm a believer in loving what you do and living the life you have always wanted.

I love shooting weddings because it allows me to do my three most FAVORITE things all in one job! I get to be outside, serve people, and create beautiful art. I strive to build relationships with my clients, bring out their goofy side, and capture them genuinely.

I LOVE to embrace awkward and make people laugh. I'm a BIG hugger and I believe in experience and kindness. My two beautiful girls and my hotty Husband give my life purpose and joy every single day. #hensonhomelife

Check out the video

Where couples dance to their own beat and heirlooms never go out of style . . .

WELCOME

Wedding Info

CHRISSY WINCHESTER PHOTOGRAPHY

🌐 CHRISSYWINCHESTER.COM

Chrissy Winchester of Chrissy Winchester Photography worked with designer Colby Stellhorn from The Coop Marketing to create a truly inviting, user friendly, and incredibly detail-oriented website. With the help of Blair Frazier of Boone & June, you will see some of the cutest and sweetest hand drawings all over the website, like little pieces of artwork in someone's home. There are so many unique elements to this website, that you will really have to head over there to appreciate them all yourself. But having an image of Chrissy's personal assistant Lily, her precious pooch, on the bottom of the contact form with the words: "Fetch Lily" is darling as well as brilliant. Chrissy wanted her online home to feel like a place where online viewers could instantly feel welcomed as friends, and she has accomplished this task masterfully.

DESIGNED BY

COLBY STELLHORN
THE COOP MARKETING

THECOOPMARKETING.COM

COLORS

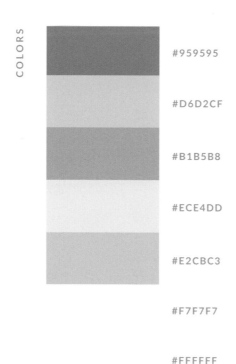

#959595

#D6D2CF

#B1B5B8

#ECE4DD

#E2CBC3

#F7F7F7

#FFFFFF

TYPEFACES

Old Standard TT Normal

Old Standard TT Italic

Cammron

Nickainley

HOME   MEET CW   PORTFOLIO   CW   WORK TOGETHER   CONTACT   BLOG

B R A N D I N G
&
L I F E S T Y L E

Photographer & (mom)preneur

IF YOU'RE HERE FOR THE SHUTTER OF MY CAMERA...

Two ways to work with Chrissy.

BRANDING
&
LIFESTYLE

Photographer & (mom)preneur

BRANDING   Ready to elevate your business aesthetic?
Let's capture the essence of your service based
business or product.

LIFESTYLE | These precious moments are fleeting. My lifestyle
photography is light, comfortable, and effortlessly
you and your family.

THE
Well Branded
STOCK SHOP

39

VELVET & WIRE

At first, her images are so stunning and displayed so elegantly, one might assume she's a photographer that hides behind her lens. But Britt Spann has no problem sharing herself with her clients. In fact, the reason her designer Courtney Malone showcased her images first, and Britt second, is exactly how the photographer treats every session: "I'm the type who invests mentally and emotionally, pouring everything that I am into every client." Britt's site, VelvetandWire.com, emphasizes just that. This online home has somehow combined a sophisticated air with an approachable uniqueness. Any potential client would feel completely at ease trusting her with their most precious moments. And they have, as Britt tells us that her website has "created a high end platform that allows me to truly reflect my brand accurately."

DESIGNED BY

courtney malone

COURTNEY MALONE CO.

COURTNEYMALONECOMPANY.COM

COLORS

#242825

#446345

#DADDD7

#967650

#9DAEAF

#F3F3F0

#ECEBE8

#FFFFFF

TYPEFACES

Oswald Normal

Merriweather Normal

Cormorant Garamond

velvet & WIRE

Fine Art photography and films told through
bold timeless, and cinematic imagery.

01. ABOUT
02. INVESTMENT
03. GALLERIES
04. BLOG
05. BOOK ME

velvet & WIRE

01. ABOUT
02. INVESTMENT
03. GALLERIES
04. BLOG
05. BOOK ME

01.
ABOUT

02
GALLERIES

velvet & WIRE

03.
INVESTMENT

.04
BOOK ME

velvet & WIRE ☰

HEY YOU, I'M BRITT.

You know that friend that loves change, speaks their mind and
isn't afraid to be 100% themselves. Well that's me. I'm that wife
that dares to take on my husband in a wrestling match and am
even convinced that one day I will beat him. I'm that mom that
makes up songs for my kids as we're driving in the car and acts
like a complete dork just to hear them laugh. I'm that stranger
who doesn't know a stranger and that person who smiles at
everyone. This is me. I'm Britt.

READ MORE

EXPLORE THE

VELVET & WIRE EXPERIENCE

V
W

You are bold, you are edgy. You are soft and you are sensuous. You
are Velvet and Wire.

TAKE ME THERE →

FLORENT VIN PHOTOGRAPHY

🌐 FLORENTVIN.COM

Florent Vin is a photographer from the South of France, shooting all over Europe and beyond. His portfolio is stacked, and so his website is the place he has chosen to showcase his best work. With one rotating hero gallery at the top of the page, there is very little to scroll down to. The inspiration for the site was "simple, basic, easy-to-understand and minimalist design", which was easy to achieve as Florent used the *Flora* design by The Design Space. But if you are looking for information, it can be found within the different headings. Florent's blog is especially interesting as he has a trove of information for his web visitors to utilize as they are searching for a photographer. From "How to find a wedding photographer" to "12 wedding photography tips for brides", Florent truly takes care of his clients from the second they see his website, to the moment he delivers their images.

DESIGNED WITH

FLORA BY THE DESIGN SPACE

COLORS

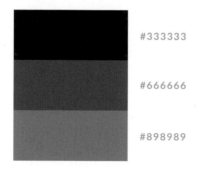

#333333

#666666

#898989

#F9F9F9

#7DA599

#DFDEDA

#ECEBE8

#FFFFFF

TYPEFACES

Cardo Normal

Cardo Italic

Lato Normal

• • •

Florent Vin

Florent Vin

≡

INSTALOVE
@florentvinphotography

BRIDES   the knot   *un Beau Jour*   fw

INSTALOVE
@florentvinphotography

© FLORENT VIN · PROVENCE · FRENCH RIVIERA · ITALY · GREECE · MONACO · PORTUGAL · SPAIN & DESTINATIONS WORLDWIDE

THE STARS INSIDE

Valentina Ring of The Stars Inside is a bright star, and you can learn all about her throughout her website, but especially in her "About Me" section. It's a lot, so be ready for your jaw to drop a few times. She has had almost every job under the sun, from an astrophysicist, to an actual circus performer, to the incredibly talented wedding planner and stylist that she is today. All this amazingness, paired with the design talents of Melissa Love from The Design Space (using the *Atelier* template), and they have created an online experience that truly allows clients to get to know Valentina and her brand up close and personally: "Every client and every professional connection has commented on how captivated they were from my website, and how strongly it gave them a sense of my brand and aesthetic style."

DESIGNED WITH

ATELIER BY THE DESIGN SPACE

COLORS

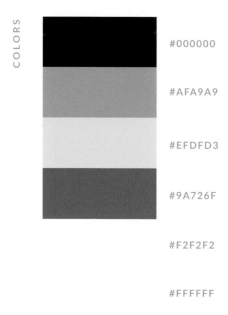

#000000

#AFA9A9

#EFDFD3

#9A726F

#F2F2F2

#FFFFFF

TYPEFACES

The Sofy Alt

Playfair Display Normal

Playfair Display Italic

OPTIMUS PRINCEPS

let yourself be
ENCHANTED

The Stars Inside is a full service wedding planning and design studio owned and run me, Valentina, for couples and creatives across the UK and Euro

This is a space for creative partnerships that bring dreamscapes and reveries to reality.
For design as artful as it is effortless, and as experiential as it is imaginative.
For thoughtful and immersive detail that transports you to another world.
For letting the light out, rather than letting outside influences in.
For aesthetic adventures with storytelling at their very core.

I believe in the power of celebrating the inner child,
of colouring outside the lines with intention.
Like you, I don't fit into boxes.
I leave room for magic.
I wonder.
I play.

Choose your own adventure ▸

THE STARS INSIDE

let yourself be
ENCHANTED.

let the
LIGHT OUT

▸ MY SERVICES
▸ PORTFOLIO
▸ WORK WITH ME

45

CREATIVE DESIGN TIPS

KELLY ZUGAY & ANDRA BARKEY
of WITH GRACE & GOLD

What is the first step you suggest to your clients when it comes to beginning the creative process for their website?

When we begin the creative process for a client's website, we first ask our clients to complete a thorough questionnaire which asks about their Ideal Client, their vision, and their goals. Then, using all they have shared, we present a proposal - a document with written and visual elements to solidify the foundation, goals, and direction of their website design. We do quite a bit of work before designing anything at all, so we can "begin with the end in mind" and know their website design has been carefully designed to achieve their unique goals.

Every brand is different, how do you help clients choose the right graphic design elements that are right for their business?

So true! Every brand is truly unique, because it is a one-of-a-kind reflection of each client's personality, style, and approach. We design our clients' brand and brand elements simultaneously, carefully creating elements which complement - and do not compete with - their work. Because each element we present has been carefully designed to align with our clients' goals, no matter which elements a client chooses, we support their choice.

For creatives just starting to design their website, can you share with us some of your favorite font pairings on the Showit platform?

PLAYFAIR DISPLAY &
LATO

MONTSERRAT &
JACQUES FRANCOIS

EB GARAMOND ITALIC &
ROBOTO LIGHT

Playfair Display

With Lato for paragraph text, these fonts create a classic combination that go together like Rachel and Ross, Lorelai and Luke, or perhaps even Elisa and Todd.

Montserrat

Parlez-vous Jacques Francois? Me neither, but isn't this pair as cute as that couple who just pulled up to the coffee shop on the Vespa with a sidecar?

EB Garamond Italic

Roboto Light, this squeeky-clean thin sans, is quite the juxtaposition to the aristocratic italic serif above. Consider the possibilities for brands that are both classic and modern.

What are some of your previous clients' color palettes that work really well together?

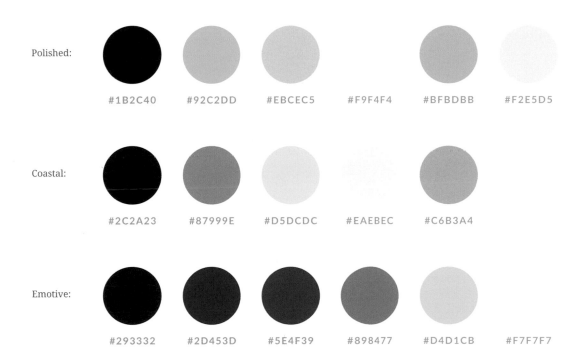

Polished: #1B2C40 #92C2DD #EBCEC5 #F9F4F4 #BFBDBB #F2E5D5

Coastal: #2C2A23 #87999E #D5DCDC #EAEBEC #C6B3A4

Emotive: #293332 #2D453D #5E4F39 #898477 #D4D1CB #F7F7F7

BENJAMIN CLIFFORD PHOTOGRAPHY

🌐 BENJAMINCLIFFORDPHOTOGRAPHY.COM

Benjamin and Joy Clifford are the husband wife photography team behind Benjamin Clifford Photography. With the help of their designer Sandra, of The Flying Muse, they created a completely customized, and totally gorgeous online home. Their breathtaking hero image grabs your attention, making website visitors eager to scroll to see more, and learn more about the photographers behind the image. The entire site is so simple and elegant as clean lines dominate but so do joyful and radiant faces. This is no stuffy gallery of beautiful images. This site is alive with Ben and Joy's heart to capture incredible images for their incredible clients. Ben says of his website: "It is a better reflection of us, our personalities, shooting style, and business. We feel our clients see that match when they visit our website and learn about us."

DESIGNED BY

SANDRA HEGEDUS
THE FLYING MUSE

THEFLYINGMUSE.CO

COLORS

#727E85

#B2BABF

#D9C1CE

#E6D5DF

#F0E7ED

#CACFD2

#FBF9F9

#FFFFFF

TYPEFACES

Vanity

Lora Normal

Playfair Display Italic

BENJAMIN CLIFFORD
PHOTOGRAPHY

WELCOME

*documenting your
wedding day is
our greatest joy!*

We provide a luxurious once-in-a-lifetime wedding photography experience for happy couples! While we are located in Phoenix, Arizona and the surrounding areas, we also travel all over! Our goal is to deliver the vision you have dreamt of your entire life.

the other side of the camera

WE PHOTOGRAPH ONCE IN A LIFETIME WEDDINGS FOR HAPPY COUPLES.

Hi there bride-to-be!
We are Ben and Joy Clifford, a husband and wife photography team. We are a couple who fell in love over 19 years ago in a small town. After dating for a very long time - 4 weeks to be exact - Ben knew she was the one and asked her to marry him. 19 years of marriage later, we're still best friends! When we are not photographing weddings, we are usually chasing around our amazing daughter, who has two different color eyes! We also love being outside soaking up the Arizona sun. Hiking, camping, fishing, and exploring new unique locations are all musts!

get to know us

featured weddings

49

CHARITY MAURER PHOTOGRAPHY

It should probably go without saying that beautiful photography is a big selling point for a photographer. Charity Maurer has that in the bag, and after teaming up with Jacki Miller of Foil & Ink, they were able to combine several different frames of rotating images as a collective that brides-to-be will be captivated by. As they continue to scroll, visitors will be not only find more gorgeous images, but so many beautifully displayed resources, as well. Charity has worked hard to build her bank of wisdom for both photographers and brides-to-be, and is happy to share it all. With help from her web designers, a list of her 5 step process, from consultation to image delivery, goes from boring "to-do" list, to engaging, interactive graphic. Charity's attention to details are represented so well in her online storefront, she can rest assured that many will be requesting her talents, as well as her peaceful presence, for their special day.

DESIGNED BY

JACKI MILLER
FOIL & INK

FOILANDINK.COM

COLORS

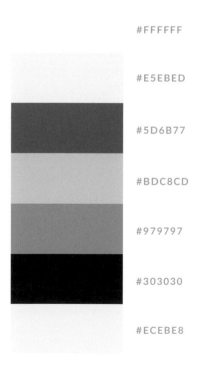

#FFFFFF

#E5EBED

#5D6B77

#BDC8CD

#979797

#303030

#ECEBE8

TYPEFACES

Nunito Normal

Nunito Ultra Light

Montserrat Light

Cormorant Normal

Cormorant Italic

Cormorant Garamond Light

CHARITY MAURER   ABOUT   GALLERIES   INFORMATION   PHOTOGRAPHERS   BLOG   INQUIRE

CM

WELCOME

Wedding Photography For Sophisticated And Luxurious Couples

PORTFOLIO

Featured Weddings

JORDAN & GREG   MADELINE & JAKE   DIANE & LOREN

☰

CHARITY MAURER

CM

WELCOME

Wedding Photography For
Sophisticated And Luxurious Couples

PORTFOLIO

Featured Weddings

ABOUT THE ARTIST

Meet Charity

With a dancer's background, I have an innate
sense for body language and visual story-telling,
and one of my life's greatest privileges is
documenting and preserving the love stories of
my clients.

Another is being wife to Andy for eight years...

51

LESLIE D PHOTOGRAPHY

🌐 LESLIEDPHOTOGRAPHY.COM

As a fine art photographer for "romantic and blissful brides" it's no wonder Leslie D enlisted the help of Jacki Miller at Foil & Ink. Her hand-illustrated logo is the perfect welcome into the blushes and florals that run through her online home, as well as Leslie's breathtaking images. Scrolling to the adorable graphs of Leslie's "About" page, visitors learn more about Leslie in an interesting and visual manner. They will also see that her favorite place to visit is Tuscany, Italy. They will instantly have the "ah-ha" moment as they recognize so many of her captures could have been taken there. Those with wanderlust and love in their hearts will feel the sense that stumbling upon LeslieDPhotography.com was the magical link to finding their dream wedding photographer.

DESIGNED BY

JACKI MILLER
FOIL & INK

FOILANDINK.COM

COLORS

#767676

#FFFFFF

#E3CABB

#F9E6D7

#FDFBF9

#C3CFCF

#ECEBE8

TYPEFACES

Cormorant Light

Cormorant Italic

new find

Open Sans Light

Oswald Light

"Named One Of The Best Arizona Wedding Photographers"

Fine Art Photography For *Romantic and Blissful* Brides.

leslie

Fine Art Photography For
Romantic and Blissful Brides.

WEDDINGS

"Leslie Doesn't Simply Take Pictures, But Truly Captures All The Emotions Of The Day. Her Amazing Skills, Warmth, And Genuine Care Is What Brings It All To Life."

Sonya + Everett

Recently Seen In

All About Our
Process

KEALA JARVIS PHOTOGRAPHY

🌐 KEALAJARVIS.COM

If the map wasn't your first clue, Keala Jarvis is an international portrait photographer. Her love for travel, only discovered in recent years, has already taken her from her home town in Utah, to an expat life in Poland. Luckily, her images have no problems transcending international barriers. Keala designed her website, KealaJarvis.com, to do the same. "My inspiration was to match the feel of collecting memories from travel, with the collage format paired with the whimsical wanderlust." The soft green, reminiscent of the sea on an old paper map, is a familiar greeting for any fellow travelers. Complete with portraits of every background and even an updated travel itinerary adding movement to the screen, Keala has found a way to make her lifestyle relatable and fun! Visitors will be sure to check back in to find out when they can cross paths with this talented, up-for-anything photographer!

DESIGNED WITH
INDIAN SUMMER BY FOIL & INK

COLORS

#FFFFFF

#C2DFCD

#DEE0DF

#414141

#000000

#DFDEDA

#ECEBE8

TYPEFACES

Karla Normal

BEBAS NEUE

Hullist

54

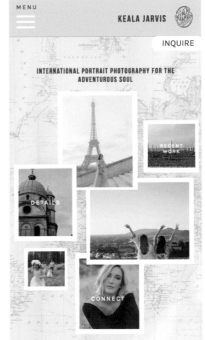

HOME   ABOUT   WORK   INQUIRE   DETAILS   SHOP   JOURNAL

INTERNATIONAL PORTRAIT PHOTOGRAPHY FOR THE ADVENTUROUS SOUL

FEATURED IN

SSG HOT 100   LEMONADE & LENSES   THE TWELFTH YEAR   BP4U MAGAZINE

Travel Dates
2018

POLAND AUGUST OCTOBER

UTAH SEPTEMBER

GERMANY NOVEMBER

AUSTRIA DECEMBER

LET'S GET SOCIAL @KEALAJPHOTO

MENU   KEALA JARVIS

INQUIRE

INTERNATIONAL PORTRAIT PHOTOGRAPHY FOR THE ADVENTUROUS SOUL

RECENT WORK

DETAILS

CONNECT

"KEALA MADE MY DAUGHTER'S SENIOR PORTRAIT DREAMS COME TRUE! KEALA TURNED THE OCCASION INTO A REMARKABLE EXPERIENCE. MY DAUGHTER LOVES HER PHOTOS! SHE WILL

A.E. GOOD PHOTOGRAPHY

🌐 AEGOODPHOTOGRAPHY.COM

Antwane and T-kia Good are the joyful photography couple behind A.E. Good Photography. "Our lives are filled with love and laughter, so we strive to make sure your images tell the same story." And this is so very evident on their website. Not just in the images, but in the copy, and in the fun colors that distinguish their brand. Using *The Erin* design by Gillian Sarah, AEGoodPhotography.com is simple, easy to navigate, and feels like you have just walked into the Goods' living room for a virtual cup of coffee. "As a new photography business in its 'brand-building' stage, having a cohesive and easy to use website has made the experience for our clients very pleasant and professional. The ease of using Showit made it possible for us as new business owners to feel confident and present our services with pride." And of course, with a smile.

DESIGNED WITH
THE ERIN BY GILLIAN SARAH

COLORS

#002B5C

#83A5DB

#FFBDB3

#30102A

#517F83

#E2E9EE

#1B1F3B

#FFFFFF

TYPEFACES

Yrsa Normal

Yrsa Light

Custom

HOME   ABOUT   INVESTMENT   **G**   GALLERIES   BLOG   CONTACT

YOUR STORY DESERVES TO BE TOLD

Beautifully & Honestly

Welcome to A.E. Good Photography. We are a husband and wife team based out of Charlotte, N.C. We have been on our life journey together for the last 14 years, praying and laughing together as we raise our family. We are so glad that you have stopped by and are excited to get to know you.

FIND OUT MORE

GALLERIES

CONTACT

THE BLOG

A.E. GOOD PHOTOGRAPHY & CO.

HOME   GALLERIES
ABOUT   BLOG
INVESTMENT   CONTACT

PHOTOGRAPHY BY ANTWANE AND T-KIA GOOD || A.E. GOOD PHOTOGRAPHY

YOUR STORY DESERVES
TO BE TOLD

Beautifully
& Honestly

Welcome to A.E. Good Photography. We

57

LAUREN ASHBY PHOTOGRAPHY

🌐 LAURENASHBYPHOTOGRAPHY.COM

Is there anyone who does not like to be greeted with a heartfelt "Hey Gorgeous"? This first impression, in a playful type, beckons the online visitor to scroll down to learn more about the creative owner of this fun site! Lauren, the photographer behind LaurenAshbyPhotography.com, captures sun-kissed images in and around Arizona. Her website is a well-thought out, intentional layout of beautiful, bright, and unique images that are at once approachable and professional. With the cleverly curated group of photos, cheeky quotes, and navigational prompts, Lauren, with the help of the bold ladies at Go Live, has set herself apart. And with a get-to-know-you quiz with a fur background, ladies of all ages will be searching her site to learn more about Lauren, as well as finding out how to contact her!

DESIGNED WITH
DUSTY ROSE BY GO LIVE

COLORS

#1A1A1A

#F8E9E4

#F1CFC5

#FB3B3B

#AEAEAE

#C9C9C9

#FFFFFF

TYPEFACES

Playfair Display Bold

Playfair Display Normal

Playfair Display Italic

PT Sans Narrow Bold

PT Sans Narrow Normal

Montserrat

hey gorgeous!

I CAPTURE SUNKISSED PORTRAIT PHOTOGRAPHY IN ARIZONA & BEYOND

hey gorgeous!

I CAPTURE SUNKISSED PORTRAIT
PHOTOGRAPHY IN ARIZONA & BEYOND

PORTFOLIO

PORTRAITS

FAMILIES

COUPLES

WEDDINGS

❝

**I was given an
immediate
confidence**

PORTFOLIO

PORTRAITS

FAMILIES

COUPLES

WEDDINGS

❝ UREN OVERDELIVERED
N EVERYTHING

DETAILS

❝

I WAS GIVEN AN IMMEDIATE
CONFIDENCE

ABOUT

CONTACT

❝

I COULD GO ON FOREVER BUT
IN SUMMARY, SHE'S JUST THE
BEST!

JULIE HAIDER

🌐 JULIEHAIDER.COM

Splashes of couples gliding through epic mountain scenery is a definitive way to let people know you are an adventurous wedding photographer. But to add in that bit of "heartfelt" and a nod to "fun" as Julie Haider describes her brand, there are several close-ups of couples looking wildly in-love in the vast wilderness. And so the only website design that would make sense for this website would be Go Live's *Alive & Free*! Julie, a born and raised adventurer, lets her potential clients know the mountains are calling, instead of a regular church, to be the sight for their impending nuptials, with illustrated peaks steering you from one portion of her website to the next. Having nature images serve as the background to various boxes of text, equally-adventurous couples will be drawn to Julie and her ability to capture love set amongst the trees.

DESIGNED WITH
ALIVE & FREE BY GO LIVE

COLORS

#454545

#404040

#0383AE

#E3BB1C

#8E8E8E

#DFDEDA

#EEEEEE

#FFFFFF

TYPEFACES

Montserrat Semi Bold

Montserrat Light

BioRhyme Light

Open Sans Light

julie haisler
ELOPEMENTS | INTIMATE WEDDINGS

HELLO | PHOTOS | INFO | TRAVEL | BLOG | CONTACT

FUN + HEARTFELT PHOTOGRAPHY FOR
ADVENTURE WEDDINGS + ELOPEMENTS

A traditional wedding isn't for
you, and neither is a typical
photographer.

Your adventurous spirits and beautiful love need to be documented by
someone who understands why you cut the guest list and moved the
wedding outside. **You need a photographer who gets you.** Let's create
photos that are authentic to you and your adventure wedding.

YES PLEASE!

Hiker. Kayaker.
National Park Geek.

Your adventure wedding is going to be super
amazing, and I can't wait to hear about it! Meet me,
and **let's see if I'm the right photographer for you!**

MEET ME!

ON THE BLOG

5 BUCKET LIST PLACES
TO ELOPE

COASTAL MAINE
ELOPEMENT INSPIRATION

TIPS FOR THE PERFECT
ELOPEMENT DRESS

GRAND TETON NATIONAL
PARK ADVENTURE SESSION

HOW TO TELL YOUR FAMILY
YOU'RE ELOPING

CALIFORNIA COAST
ELOPEMENT INSPIRATION

julie haisler
ELOPEMENTS | INTIMATE WEDDINGS

FUN + HEARTFELT PHOTOGRAPHY FOR
**ADVENTURE
WEDDINGS + ELOPEMENTS**

A traditional wedding
isn't for you, and neither
is a typical photographer.

PATTY JESSEE PHOTOGRAPHY

🌐 PATTYJESSEE.COM

Patty of Patty Jessee Photography worked with designer and brand strategist Julie Story to create the bold and vibrant PattyJessee.com. With punches of gold on a black and white background, the images and heart of Patty Jessee really stand out. As you dig further into the website, you also find Brooke, Patty's daughter, who makes up the Newborn department of the business, while Patty focuses primarily on the Seniors. Their tag line: "Personalities as art, from tiny toes to senior glows" is truly what these two photographers are about! They sincerely believe that the work that they do can change a life. There's even a video on their website from a mom whose son passed away who really drives that point home. The images that Patty took are the ones she has in her home, and they truly leave a lasting legacy.

COLORS

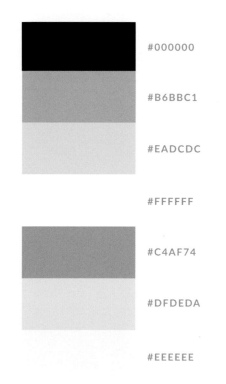

#000000

#B6BBC1

#EADCDC

#FFFFFF

#C4AF74

#DFDEDA

#EEEEEE

TYPEFACES

Playfair Display Normal

Montserrat Light

faith and glory

PATTY*jessee*

HOME   ABOUT   OUR WORK   INFO   INVEST   CONTACT

CAN ONE IMAGE
CHANGE YOUR LIFE?

•

we believe it can

FIND OUT HOW

CAPTURING YOUR CHILDREN'S AUTHENTICITY, ONE *personality* AT A TIME

MEET
PATTY

mother, photographer, authenticity seeker

IMAGES CAN CHANGE YOU.
take our word for it... but also...
TAKE HERS.....

AFTER WILL'S HEARTBREAKING DEATH, SEE
HOW THESE IMAGES CHANGED EVERYTHING....
watch the full video ▶

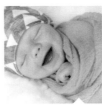

GET THE DETAILS *babies*

GET THE DETAILS *seniors*

PERSONALITIES AS ART
tiny toes to senior glam

PATTY*jessee*

CAN ONE IMAGE
CHANGE YOUR LIFE?
•
we believe it can
FIND OUT HOW

CAPTURING YOUR CHILDREN'S AUTHENTICITY, ONE *personality* AT A TIME

MEET
PATTY

mother, photographer, authenticity seeker

▼

IMAGES CAN CHANGE YOU.
take our word for it... but also...
TAKE HERS.....

63

TOMAYIA COLVIN PHOTOGRAPHY

 TOMAYIACOLVIN.COM

Pops of pink and lots of moving pieces help capture the attention of website visitors who are looking for a skillful and fun photographer. With the help of Katie Loerts Graphic Design, TomayiaColvin.com is a full brand experience! Bunking the idea that a white background is boring, Katie and Tomayia merged their skills and made her brand images pop off the screen. She took her branding a step further than the average (because Tomayia is far above average) by having her site, logo, and even what she wore to her brand shoot, to match completely. Add this to her streamlined font and design and it's easy to see that Tomayia leaves no detail unattended to. Whether her visitor is a couple, high school senior, or even a blossoming new photographer, her ideal client is as bold and bright as this website, and the photographer behind it all.

DESIGNED BY

KATIE
LOERTS
GRAPHIC DESIGN

KATIE LOERTS GRAPHIC DESIGN

KATIELOERTSDESIGN.COM

COLORS

#E971A6

#3C3D41

#F0B3CE

#90794F

#F7F1F2

#E3E4DF

#FFFFFF

#000000

TYPEFACES

Horley

HorleyItalic

SpartanThin

Montserrat

TOMAYIA COLVIN
PHOTOGRAPHY

TAKE A PEEK AT MY #1 AMAZON BEST SELLING BOOK!

just you.

"

TOMAYIA IS ONE OF THE 50 MOST
INSPIRING
PHOTOGRAPHERS
IN THE UNITED STATES."

Beauty Revived

TOMAYIA COLVIN
PHOTOGRAPHY

just you.

"

**TOMAYIA IS ONE OF
THE 50 MOST**
INSPIRING
PHOTOGRAPHERS
IN THE UNITED STATES."

PHILOSOPHY

Tomayia Colvin Photography believes that high school
seniors, regardless of where they come from, should have the
opportunity to experience a portrait session that makes you
feel good and look amazing!

Our Houston High School Senior Sessions, Wedding, and
Engagement Sessions are designed to show off what makes
you special. You can find us in the Humble,
Kingwood, Atascocita, and Greater Houston area.
Always having fun and giving our clients the
ultimate Tomayia Colvin experience.

"

TOMAYIA IS AN AMAZING PHOTOGRAPHER,
SHE HAS A TREMENDOUS TALENT OF
CAPTURING EVERY DETAIL
OF THE EVENT BEAUTIFULLY. SHE TRULY LOVES WHAT SHE
DOES AND IT IS EVIDENT IN EVERY PICTURE SHE TAKES."

Dextor R.

HEY THERE, I'M TOMAYIA!

Tomayia Colvin is a nationally published High School Senior Portrait
Photographer in Houston that specializes in carefree, funky, and real
portrait sessions that bring out the best in you – both inside and out. We
hand-select all of our products to ensure that you will be taking home
museum quality pieces and sharing thoughtful keepsakes with friends
and family. You can find us in the Humble, Kingwood, Atascocita, and

ERIN JACHIMIAK PHOTOGRAPHY

🌐 ERINJACHIMIAK.COM

There is no doubt in anyone's mind that Erin Jachimiak is a photographer for moms: she calls her website visitors "Mama," and her logo is a cute little lamb with a red bow! Her brand and website speak fluent "Mom," thanks to her amazing designer Moriah Riona, but the heartbeat of the website is all Erin's. "I really want to encourage women to love the things that their bodies are capable of, and to cherish and remember all of the moments - they are fleeting." Erin describes her ideal clients as: "a mama or mama to be, seeking a luxury portrait experience different from the normal cookie cutter portrait studios." Considering that Erin's website is not a cookie cutter experience, her web visitors know they are in the right place. The copy, the images, and that bow-tied lamb all help tell a memorable story that really sets Erin and her website apart.

DESIGNED BY

MORIAH RIONA
MORIAH RIONA BRANDING

MORIAHRIONA.COM

COLORS

#212121

#BDDBD1

#E9E4D7

#A4793D

#589EA0

#C92C2D

#858585

#FFFFFF

TYPEFACES

Roboto Bold

Roboto Medium

Roboto Slab Bold

Roboto Slab Normal

Lora Normal

Celebrating
MOTHERHOOD

YOUR GREATEST ACCOMPLISHMENT

You created this amazing, beautiful new life in YOUR body and that deserves to be celebrated. Once you set foot in my studio, you will forget about the chaos and confusion that is your life right now.

I create a truly one of a kind portrait experience for each and every client. Let's honor you and celebrate this amazing little human that gets to call you Mom.

LET'S CELEBRATE YOU!

erin jachimiak
PHOTOGRAPHY

Celebrating

MOTHERHOOD

YOUR GREATEST ACCOMPLISHMENT

You created this amazing, beautiful new life in YOUR body and that deserves to be celebrated. Once you set foot in my studio, you will forget about the chaos and confusion that is your life

HEY THERE, MAMA!

I'm Erin.
....

I'm a mom – just like you! I know, first-hand, how overwhelming new parenthood can be. I know what it's like to be caring for a new family and and to always put yourself last.

I'm here to put you first. To help you to forget about everything else — and capture this one perfect moment (amidst all the chaos!).

Let's celebrate you and your beautiful new family!

| HAPPY CLIENTS |

ERIN IS ABSOLUTELY FANTASTIC!!

We have had the pleasure of working with her two times already and on each occasion she is been more than accommodating, creative, fun and has captured absolutely wonderful memories for us. We cannot wait to share many more sessions with her as our family photographer.

JENNY B.

Featured
PORTRAIT EXPERIENCES

MALAK

Dreamy Colorado Mountain
Maternity Experience

JOZEE

In-Studio Newborn Experience
With The Whole Family

JACK

Playful & Colorful In-Studio
Sitter Experience

AZAIFA

Sweet & Snuggly Newborn
Studio Experience

ON-BRAND COPYWRITING

with ASHLYN CARTER

Why is good copywriting so important when building your website?

In a nutshell, copywriting is the art and science of your brand's voice on purpose. We get so caught up, I think, in the beautiful visuals of marketing, and I get it! That stuff is so fun. BUT, copywriting is a paramount piece when it comes to marketing sales (hello! The thing we need to run businesses!), both online and offline.

Your visuals and your designs pique interest, but it's really your copy that converts the buyer. Tells your story. Makes the sell. While 90% (some studies say 93%) of information is digested visually, simply put, copywriting and on-brand imagery have GOT to work in tandem together to round everything out. It's paramount.

Words hold hefty weight simply because story still matters—it always will for humans!—and imagery alone doesn't always communicate the full story. You've probably felt this tension if you've sat down and struggled with what to say for your website, about page, or sales copy.

Are you writing to represent your brand or are you trying to appeal more to your ideal client?

Both. First of all, the best copy isn't in your head—it's probably in your ideal client's head—so we just have to "get over ourselves" in a way and quit getting so caught up in figuring out our voice. That's important, but it's just as important to appeal to your ideal client.

What I teach my students is that it's a Venn diagram: one circle is YOUR voice, your message, your mission, and one circle is your ideal client's words, problems, and mission. Where those two circles overlap, that is the copy you want to use in your sales and marketing. You want to target your copy to your ideal client while keeping your brand voice on point.

If you have that ideal client researched to a "T," you're well on your way to selling authentically to him or her. From there, it's simple: Now that you know your client (meaning you also know his or her external, internal, and psychological problems), it's just a matter of weaving that into your brand messaging. It's just speaking to him or her.

For more visual creatives that don't like to write, do you suggest outsourcing? How do I know that it will sound like me?

Nope. Not at first at least. This is one thing I get a little soapboxy about. So many creatives hear about copywriting for the first time, and get jazzed: "WHAT!? You mean I don't have to do this!? Awesome, let me hand it off." I get that. I do. But the problem here is that so many times, you're inadvertently outsourcing the sales psychology that you NEED to understand as the CEO and CMO of your creative small business.

You know how at first you have to kinda learn how to run your numbers, even if you hate math? Emoji hand raised here—bookkeeping was my nemesis! But, as someone who outsources that now, I get it. I have a framework to understand what my bookkeeper's doing and how to understand my PnLs.

Copywriting is (at least when done by someone who really gets it!) not a flippant investment. That's another reason why I feel really passionate about this. Stewardship of our time, treasure, and resources is so important, and I don't think that four-figure money should be spent until a copywriter can honestly tell you they can make your investment back for you. That usually isn't the case until you've been in business for a bit, learned your market, and learned your product. My best, top-dollar launch clients still write so much of their own copy. I honestly feel like copy should be one of the later things you outsource. You need to be on website 3.0. You need to have been in business for a while, solidified your offerings, and know your audience incredibly well.

I also say it a lot when I speak, but if you can't tell me—again, as the CEO—why you do what you do the way you do different OR better than someone who offers something similar, we need to camp out there. You need to be able to communicate that to me. To anyone. That's your unique selling proposition. Think about *Shark Tank*—the minute an entrepreneur goes on that show and can't make the pitch about what they do and why it's worthy of someone's time and money, they're dead in the water. It's not about being the best salesman, it's just about being a good communicator, which, again, is a business skill that isn't going anywhere.

I'm on a bit of a mission you could say to get that message out. Ha! Hiring the pros is a GOOD thing, but I wouldn't recommend starting there. I really do want to make copywriting less of this esoteric, professionals-only club and help teach creative small business owners how they can DIY so much of it. Hopefully, that's what I've been able to do on my YouTube channel, blog, and shop.

How do you make your copywriting feel personal and fun but also professional?

While you may have a "mood board" for your brand's color palette, photo direction, and logo, you may not have a moodboard for your brand voice and sound. I want you to have a nailed-down brand voice that helps you write copy that lets your reader or target dream client "hear" you before they hire you, and that's where it can be fun! I think we get really caught up on voice … for example, I see a lot of my clients and students think if they want to market to a high-end, luxury market, they have to change their voice to this Mercedes-coming-around-the-bend-golf-announcer voice. That's not it. Remember what I said—it's that Venn diagram visual.

I created a quiz a while back to help creatives find their online voice vibe, and hopefully, it's a fun reminder that this should not be so serious. Yes, it has research based in personal types behind it (and that's serious!), but the questions, the delivery of the results … all that was created to remind us that marketing can be fun. It can be voicey. Finding your brand voice is a matter of applying what you know about yourself as the face of your business to what that gap is in the market that you're speaking to.

You can take the quiz here: ashlynwrites.com/quiz

LITTLE STORIES - THE MOMENT BY AMY

🌐 LITTLE-STORIES.CO

They aren't photos as much as they are visual narratives that in every way live up to their namesake domain, Little-Stories.co. The photographer who creates these images, Amy Law, finds deep inspiration from relationships as well as art and nature. These three concepts sweep through her online home as visitors weave in and out of quietly inviting galleries, your click serving as a door to another book of tales. Sam and Rachel at Northfolk & Co were the perfect designers for Amy to pair with, setting the stage for Amy's work to shine. Website visitors will give up their "potential client" status in seconds to click "Contact Me" quickly. Each new client, waiting with eager anticipation for their story to be immortalized through the great story telling eyes of Amy Law, and maybe even featured on her brilliant site.

DESIGNED BY

SAMANTHA CULP & RACHEL THATCHER
NORTHFOLK & CO

NORTHFOLK.CO

COLORS

#4F5258

#A9A198

#FBF5F3

#D3CBC6

#FFFFFF

#B2A7AA

#EDD1C6

TYPEFACES

Josefin Sans Bold

Josefin Sans Light

Meliha Letter

Cormorant Normal

Bodoni FLF

little stories

THE MOMENT BY AMY

FINE ART PHOTOGRAPHY

I	II	III	IV	V	VI	VII
HOME	GALLERY	JOURNAL	BLOG	BIO	KIND WORDS	INQUIRE

Browse Our Galleries

01 ENGAGEMENT

02 FASHION

03 KIDS

little stories

THE MOMENT BY AMY

FINE ART PHOTOGRAPHY

Browse Our Galleries

from the
JOURNAL

FEATURE 1
PORTRAIT

FEATURE 2
COUPLE

FEATURE 3
ENGAGEMENT

View the Journal

VISIBLE BY HANNAH

🌐 VISIBLEBYHANNAH.COM

Unlike most websites, VisibleByHannah.com will not be confined to an angular protocol. Open circle graphics subtly apply movement to this clean site. Because Hannah's brand images are so personal and inviting, visitors may not notice the delightful elliptic theme immediately. Of course, designer Sarah Shuttle of Orla knew this would further underscore Hannah's unique brand statement of making "your brand VISIBLE in the most beautiful and natural way." With over a decade of photography and marketing under her belt, Hannah knows how to convey a brand message. And her desire to do it in a "holistic approach to how your images fit in your wider marketing needs," is the exact thing her website conveys. Hannah McClune has found the way to communicate her brand visually, and it's easy to see that she will be doing the same for many who visit her website.

DESIGNED BY

SARAH SHUTTLE
ORLA

SARAHSHUTTLE.COM

COLORS

#000000

#4D4D4D

#DFDFDF

#F9F5F1

#EFE3DD

#F1F1F1

#979797

#FFFFFF

TYPEFACES

Libre Baskerville Italic

Sweet Sans Regular

Sweet Sans Medium

Visible
BY HANNAH

SERVICES

PORTFOLIO

EXPERIENCE

THE BLOG

CONTACT

Make your brand VISIBLE in the most beautiful and natural way.

High quality images set the right tone with a professional look, you can give your business a personality that fits your brand. The lifestyle approach to the photos makes your brand relatable; people love to see what you do and how you are an expert in your field.

Attract customers you love with bespoke visual content

Brand photography gives you an authentic visual presence to attract your ideal audience. You can use your images to build relationships with your dream clients and encourage engagement with your brand.

Telling your brand's visual story

I'm Hannah, a full time photographer based in Reading, Berkshire. I create clean, modern and feminine images for small business owners.

More than a photographer. A MARKETING EXPERT.

Before becoming a photographer in 2011 I worked in marketing. My role involved commissioning photo shoots- from the concept and briefing, to using the resulting images in global campaigns. My fifteen years experience means I have a holistic approach to how your images fit in your wider marketing needs.

Tell Me More

Visible
BY HANNAH

lifestyle brand photography

Make your brand VISIBLE in the most beautiful and natural way.

High quality images set the right tone with a professional look, you can give your business a personality that fits your brand. The lifestyle approach to the photos makes your brand relatable; people love to see what you

... the photographs are even more beautiful than I could have imagined...

- VICTORIA LUMBERLEGE, ETERNAL
BLOOMS BY VICTORIA

LIEB PHOTOGRAPHIC

🌐 LIEBPHOTOGRAPHIC.COM

Facts are better remembered in a story as opposed to facts stated on their own. For example, here's a fact: Michelle Lieb of Lieb Photographic is a supremely talented photographer. When you visit her website, you can see evidence of this fact in the unforgettable stories told in her pictures. These stories, told in a triad of images, are unique and visually stunning. Michelle is an artist in so many regards (watercolor or photographic), and she really created something amazing digitally—her website. Starting off with the *Positano* design by the Palm Shop, Michelle masterfully customized the perfect clean and classic canvas for her art. Finding her niche in romantic weddings and lifestyle fine art photography, her work really jumps off the white background, and leaves an impression. This truly memorable experience on Michelle's website, LiebPhotographic.com, has been easily converting visitors into dream clients since it's launch.

DESIGNED WITH
POSITANO BY DAVEY & KRISTA

COLORS

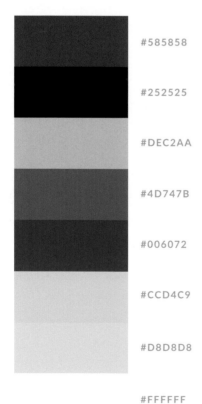

#585858

#252525

#DEC2AA

#4D747B

#006072

#CCD4C9

#D8D8D8

#FFFFFF

TYPEFACES

Cormorant Garamond Italic

Cormorant Garamond Normal

Montserrat Light

LIEB PHOTOGRAPHIC

with Michelle Lieb

classic, joyful, romantic

SLIDE | 01 02 03 04 05

Visit the galleries to see more work →

SLIDE | 01 02 03 04 05

Visit the galleries to see more work →

HEY THERE FRIENDS!

WELCOME AND HELLO!

Meet Michelle of Lieb Photographic

HEY THERE FRIENDS!

WELCOME AND HELLO!

Hello, I'm Michelle!

VIRGINIA BASED WEDDING & LIFESTYLE PHOTOGRAPHER

Welcome to a place where love is cherished, memories are treasured and sentimental hearts are understood. Welcome to a place where one of the best days of your life will be honored, respected and joyfully celebrated with you. I understand that planning a wedding is one of the most exciting things you will ever plan. I want to make this part of your process fun, simple and enjoyable. My heart is to give you an incredible photographic experience from beginning to end.

GET TO KNOW ME

the
TESTIMONIALS
WHAT CLIENTS AND WEDDING PROFESSIONALS ARE SAYING

CURRENTLY ON THE BLOG |

READ THE MOST RECENT BLOG!

READ THE POST

the
FEATURES
SEE WHERE MY WORK HAS BEEN FEATURED

fun in your inbox!
JOIN THE LIST

EMAIL ADDRESS

TERRI BASKIN PHOTOGRAPHY

🌐 TERRIBASKIN.COM

The marriage between a bride and a groom is always so beautiful to witness, but how about the union of an incredible photographer and equally amazing designers? That's what you have before you here. Terri Baskin shoots stylish, classy, and fun brides and grooms. And this is because Terri is all of those things, and so is her website! "My website validates my brand and my client experience and showcases my professionalism for current and potential clients." Designers Davey and Krista Jones did a phenomenal job of transferring all that is Terri, into TerriBaskin.com. Instead of being overwhelmed at all the information and expertise Terri has to offer, they were able to organize all the resources into a streamlined, and informative website. So whether you are looking to hire her, or you are in need of educational resources, visitors will be happy to stop their search, stay, and learn something new.

DESIGNED BY

DAVEY & KRISTA JONES

DAVEYANDKRISTA.COM

COLORS

#585858

#252525

#E4D2C1

#FEEFEA

#C5A97D

#FEEFEB

#D8D8D8

#FFFFFF

TYPEFACES

Montserrat Normal

Montserrat Light

Didot

Didot Italic

Styled Edit

TERRI BASKIN
PHOTOGRAPHY

QUICK LINKS: 01 *The Wedding Experience*   02 *View the Portfolio*   03 *Engagement Session Q&A*   04 *Ready to Book?*

Meet Terri

I believe my clients deserve my full attention not only on their wedding day, but up until their day. I also believe that your wedding day should be your dream day coming to life, and that your love should shine through for all of your friends and family to see. My goal is to capture that authentic love and emotion between you and your new spouse.

What I love most about weddings is the look on the groom's face when he sees his bride for the first time. Sometimes I photograph tears and other times I photograph the nervous laughter of all the months of planning finally coming to fruition. Either way it goes, I am here to document it all!

LEARN MORE

TERRI BASKIN
PHOTOGRAPHY

QUICK LINKS:

From the Clients

"TERRI MADE US FEEL LIKE WE WERE NATURALS"

STEPHEN & ARIEL, MARRIED 2017

Choose your
EXPERIENCE

NEWLY ENGAGED?

learn about my engagement sessions and pricing

LEARN MORE

PREPARING FOR "I DO"?

The Wedding Experience - Details, Pricing, Booking

LEARN MORE

I'M A CREATIVE OR A PHOTOGRAPHER

My favorite tools, upcoming engagements, and see how we help

LEARN MORE

KARA KNAPP PHOTOGRAPHY

🌐 KARAKNAPP.COM

Some people have dealt with a lot in life, but instead of letting that drag them down, they use that as fuel to passionately serve others. This is the heart of Kara Knapp Photography. She shares some of the hardships she has endured on her website because it is the "why" behind her business. Kara not only does this in words, but does this so beautifully in her visual brand as well. The photographer describes her style as "soft, timeless, and organic." By starting with a design from The Palm Shop by Davey & Krista Jones as her foundation, Kara has built an inviting, beautiful, and sweet online home for herself. As a Newborn and Lifestyle Photographer, her story draws clients in, but her work speaks for itself. Ultimately Kara's "why" is the exact reason her clients choose her over and over again for every moment needing capturing in their lives.

DESIGNED WITH
BETHANY BY DAVEY & KRISTA

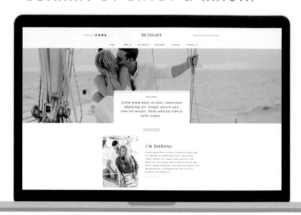

COLORS

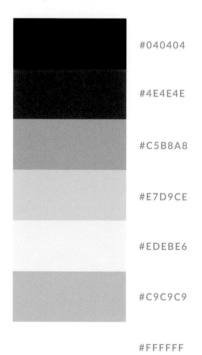

#040404

#4E4E4E

#C5B8A8

#E7D9CE

#EDEBE6

#C9C9C9

#FFFFFF

TYPEFACES

Libre Baskerville Normal

Libre Baskerville Italic

Montserrat Normal

Volstead

OLDSTYLE CAPS

Old Style

Oldstyle Italic

WELCOME

Hello Friend!

My name is Kara and I'm the one behind the
camera here at Kara Knapp Photography. I was
born in North Carolina, raised in Texas, and
moved to Arizona after saying 'I do' to my
favorite guy. I'm a lover of (decaf!) iced coffee,
long talks, good books, and any time spent with
family and friends. Target is my weakness, I can't
dance, but I love to, and home is my favorite
place to be.

learn more »

LATEST

CLAIRE VICTORIA   EMMA TURNS ONE   LUNDEN TURNS ONE
LIFESTYLE NEWBORN SESSION   MILESTONE SESSION   MILESTONE SESSION

THE FULL STORY »   THE FULL STORY »   THE FULL STORY »

INSTAGRAM

ME ON 🅾 f p      Kara Knapp is a lifestyle
photographer based in Phoenix,
Arizona. She specializes in
newborns, maternity, and family
photography.

© 2017 Kara Knapp Photography
Photos by Kara Knapp │ Design by The Palm Shop │ Powered by Shauti S

Kara Knapp
PHOTOGRAPHY & LIFESTYLE   ☰

WELCOME

KAT BOOGAARD

🌐 KATBOOGAARD.COM

As a freelance writer, Kat Boogaard needed her online presence to be professional but still fun and approachable. Combining her writing abilities with Rachael Earl's design skills, the two creatives came up with a fun brand and website, balancing her need to attract potential clients to hire her, and new freelance writers looking for tips and tricks on how to burst onto the scene. With Kat taking care of all the engaging copy, Rachael got working on illustrations of cute pens and pencils with tiny scattered paper clips serving as the background to drive home the visual message of what Kat offers to her audience. With a playful yet sensible color palette, clients will find it easy to trust Kat with their writing assignments, or as an online mentor in hopes of following in her footsteps as a "six-figure freelance writer."

DESIGNED BY

RACHAEL EARL
RACHAEL EARL DESIGN

RACHAELEARL.COM

COLORS

#292C2F

#C9C9C9

#364451

#8C9BA2

#EDAE9D

#BFD5D2

#F5F4F0

#FFFFFF

TYPEFACES

Cormorant SC Normal

Cormorant Garamond Italic

Libre Baskerville Normal

Libre Baskerville Italic

kat boogaard

MENU

hi there, friends

Are you wondering what *exactly* it is I do here? Well…

Ugh. That dreaded "tell me about yourself" question. I'll be honest: I always struggle to explain what I do for a living. The short answer is that I'm a freelance writer. No, that doesn't mean I'm home in my sweatpants writing the next great romance novel (alright, you caught me—I'm probably in my sweatpants). Instead, I focus mainly on crafting online content related to careers, productivity, entrepreneurship, and self-development. Whew! I guess that wasn't so hard.

GET TO KNOW ME BETTER »

Writing is my job, but educating is my passion. I'm lucky enough to get to do both every single day.

Writing for my clients is what pays my bills (and I'm also one of the fortunate ones who actually loves my day job). Are you ready for the not-so-humble brag?

You may have seen my byline a variety of places, including Forbes, Fast Company, TIME, Inc., Business Insider, The Muse, Trello, Mashable, and more.

When I'm not doing that? Here's what's really sets me off into a rather obnoxious happy dance: Using my own insights and experiences to create different resources that help other creative freelancers start and grow their own bomb-diggity businesses. Through my blog, newsletter, digital downloads, Facebook community, and more, I love helping freelancers take that leap and build lives and careers they adore. Alright, that's enough—I'm gettin' all misty-eyed over here.

FEATURED PROJECTS

the portfolio

4 Lessons I Learned From Quitting My Job With No Back-up Plan

The 1 Quick Question That Will Instantly Make You More Productive

MORE FEATURED WORK »

YOU MAY HAVE SEEN ME…

JOIN THE FREELANCE COMMUNITY ON FACEBOOK »

MENU

kat boogaard

hi there, friends

Are you wondering what *exactly* it is I do here? Well…

Ugh. That dreaded "tell me about yourself" question. I'll be honest: I

AMBER LEA PHOTOGRAPHY

🌐 AMBERLEAPHOTOS.COM

Although this husband and wife wedding photography team is based in Tuscon, Arizona, Jon and Amber Lea Russel's images could easily have their visitors guessing they shoot solely at Italian villas. With the help of designer Rachael Earl, the romantic *Rendezvous* template from Tonic Site Shop was heavily customized to tell a stunningly beautiful story with their images and Amber's words. With elegant touches, like their modern and luxurious logo, the brilliant font combinations, and the soft color palette, their website really speaks to their ideal clients. And while their goal is to capture clients' weddings in a timeless and classic style, they also want to help write their love story. "Composing our story has taught us how to write yours." Any couple that is truly in love and happens upon AmberLeaPhotos.com will be excited to have Jon and Amber be the co-authors of their big day.

CUSTOMIZED BY

RACHAEL EARL
RACHAEL EARL DESIGN

RACHAELEARL.COM

COLORS

#000000

#869F9A

#808284

#FAF5F2

#90744F

#939597

#E0E6E6

#FFFFFF

TYPEFACES

COPPERPLATE LIGHT

Brandon Grotesque Regular

Baskerville

Adagio Pro

AMBER LEA
FAITH LOVE HOPE

HOME   ABOUT   PORTFOLIO   INVESTMENT   CONTACT   BLOG

Welcome

We are Jon and Amber Lea Russell, a Tucson, Arizona based husband and wife photography team, available for travel worldwide.

SPECIALIZING IN
WEDDINGS & LIFESTYLE
PORTRAITURE

ELEGANT | TIMELESS | INTIMATE

Socialize

AMBER LEA
FAITH LOVE HOPE

Tucson, Arizona Wedding Photographers

JON & AMBER LEA RUSSELL

Our photography is an ever evolving love letter to each other. Each milestone, each accomplishment; a loving flourish, crafted together. This is our love story. Composing our story has taught us how to write yours. Amber Lea started the business, but truth be told, it has always been a joint effort. In fact, for 12 years Jon has always been within arm's reach. Sometimes he is next to me, holding my hand as we adventure together. Other days he is in front, leading me through storms and trials. The days I need him most, you'll see him behind me. Pushing me toward my dreams, and catching me when I fall. But through it all, it is always the two of us. Together.

MORE ABOUT US »

THE LATEST
On the Blog

RETURN TO TOP

DAMIEN CARTER PHOTOGRAPHY

🌐 DAMIENCARTERPHOTOGRAPHY.COM

Damien has every intention of putting his best foot forward at all times. So when it came to his first online impression, he went all out. Working with Erica Clayton at Refinery Original, he was able to combine his professionalism, with his heart for his clients. A leather detail and suited images of the photographer reminds you of his attention to detail, while a quick glance at his copy allows the prospective client to know his heart. "When I am your wedding photographer I don't want the fun to stop there. I want to be there for other special moments in your life, ... from maternity and senior pics. If it is special to you, then I want to capture it and preserve it." Perfectly balancing his professionalism with his compassionate heart to serve his client, Damien has found the exact visual balance to reflect his core values through his online storefront.

DESIGNED BY

ERICA CLAYTON
REFINERY ORIGINAL

REFINERYORIGINAL.COM

COLORS

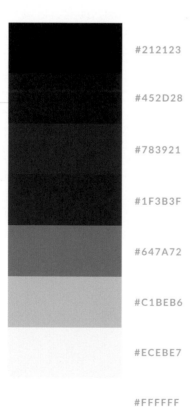

#212123

#452D28

#783921

#1F3B3F

#647A72

#C1BEB6

#ECEBE7

#FFFFFF

TYPEFACES

Oswald Normal

Oswald Light

Old Standard TT Normal

Old Standard TT Italic

Avenir Next

ENGRAVERS

Est. 2013

DAMIEN CARTER

WEDDINGS | PHOTOGRAPHY | PORTRAITS

SERVING YOU ON THE GREATEST DAY OF YOUR LIFE

I am a wedding and lifestyle photographer serving clients in the Washington DC area. I love to capture special moments for clients and I strive to leave you with lasting memories that truly capture the essence of YOU. I have photographed families and portraits since 2010 and I began to shoot weddings in 2013.

Once I got that wedding bug I couldn't let it go. Being a part of milestones in your life and being able to preserve them for you is an honor and a privilege for me. When you choose me as your photographer the things I can guarantee are a great eye for storytelling and great images.

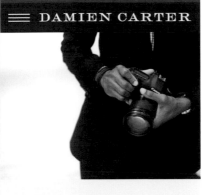

DAMIEN CARTER

Est. 2013

Damien Carter

WEDDINGS | PHOTOGRAPHY | PORTRAITS

SERVING YOU ON THE GREATEST DAY OF YOUR LIFE

I am a wedding and lifestyle photographer serving clients in the Washington DC area. I love to capture special moments for clients and I strive to leave you with lasting memories that truly capture the essence

....

I believe in love and capturing life's special moments from your wedding day onto your family portraits.

TESTIMONIALS
KAMIA

The professionalism and attention to detail were flawless. The final product was above and beyond what I could have envisioned...the best portraits I have ever received from a professional photographer.

WEDDINGS

THE BIG DAY!

So much love, laughter and joy. But the truth is, it goes by in a blink. You have spent so much time planning the perfect day but when you are in it, the hard part is taking it all in. You should hire a photographer that will pay attention to the details and I am not just talking about the cake and the dress on a hook.

I look for the Big moments AND the small moments in between. I am inspired by the love stories I get to capture and it really energizes me every single time I prepare for wedding days. Contact me for a free 15 minute consultation to see if we are a good fit.

VIEW THE PORTFOLIO

LIFESTYLE

K E DYER PHOTOGRAPHY

🌐 KEDYERPHOTOGRAPHY.COM

Elegant and sophisticated, with an air of relatability is not an easy task to pull off. However, Krystal Dyer successfully struck the chord between classic and warm on her website to further emphasize her photographic style. Adding her own point of view on a traditional portrait session, Krystal reiterates her elegant brand with her choices in color and font for her online home while also adding a twist of modern flair. Using the *Mary Kate* design by Ribbon & Ink, Krystal broke up her galleries into her three offerings, directing potential clients right to their desired section so as not to overwhelm. The simple elegance of KEDyerPhotography.com is a smart approach to giving visitors exactly what they are looking for—a fabulous photographer who knows how valuable her clients' time and attention are.

DESIGNED WITH

MARY KATE BY RIBBON & INK

COLORS

#A19D9D

#E8D4CD

#F0E1D5

#DDDDDD

#EBEBEB

#DFD9CE

#E7E7DD

#FFFFFF

TYPEFACES

Homemade Apple

Lora

Lora Italic

MEET YOUR PHOTOGRAPHER   FOR THOSE SEEKING A   follow kcdp on instagram
—Krystal Dyer   PERSONALIZED PORTRAIT   @kedyerphotography
                   EXPERIENCE

MEET YOUR PHOTOGRAPHER >>
Krystal Dyer

I'm a portrait and wedding photographer located in the West Georgia area. I'm a wife, mom, and amateur (but enthusiastic) cupcake baker. I absolutely love to capture moments, in a natural light setting, that are otherwise forgotten. Life seems to fly by, so my ultimate goal is to capture that moment for you to cherish for a lifetime.

I'm a full service photographer, which means I offer an array of products such as prints, albums, cards, and announcements just to name a few.

When I'm not at a photography session you can find me baking cupcakes, shopping at Target (finding something I don't need), drinking a white chocolate mocha from Starbucks, or getting food recipes off of Pinterest.

I'm so very excited to get started with your incredible story!

·· a few of my faves

INVESTMENT

PORTRAITS

Capture every single moment. We all know life seems to zoom by. I encourage you to take a moment and schedule your session to capture these amazing moments in your life. There's a story in every photo session and I'd love to tell yours!

Each session is uniquely planned to fit your style. I like to describe your experience with me as a "one stop shop." I'm with you the entire time to plan, select products during your in home session reveal, down to the delivery.

Families, Seniors, Maternity - 1 hour
$175 Session Fee

Newborn - 2 hours
$225 Session Fee

*Prints/Digitals sold separately

WEDDINGS

It's time to plan your upcoming wedding! i love to capture weddings and all of the beautiful emotions during the day! I include a planning session before the wedding, so we'll be ready to focus on what's most important to you! To ensure each of my wedding clients get the ultimate photography experience, I accept a limited number of weddings per year.

Out of state or destination wedding? Let's chat!!!

Wedding collections start at $1700

FOR THOSE SEEKING A PERSONALIZED PORTRAIT EXPERIENCE

GALLERIES

VJBURGOS PHOTOGRAPHY

🌐 VJBURGOSPHOTOGRAPHY.COM

As a lifestyle and wedding photographer, Valerie Burgos of VJBurgos Photography loves to serve her clients well by allowing them to enjoy their momentous occasions, while she does the heavy lifting. She is even respectful of everyone's time by allowing website visitors to see if Val is the right photographer for them, but also if they are the right clients for Val. The "VJB Brand Elements" section is the place where this happens. Here, future clients can actually see if THEY are represented in these images: from beautiful blooms, to sparkles, to sweet treats. How great is that? Val says of her website: "It has helped me stand out, and helped my customers fall in love with my brand and my work a lot more." She used the gorgeous *Everly* design by Seaside Creative to create a clean, and simple to navigate website, which her web visitors undoubtedly also appreciate.

DESIGNED WITH
EVERLY BY SEASIDE CREATIVE

COLORS

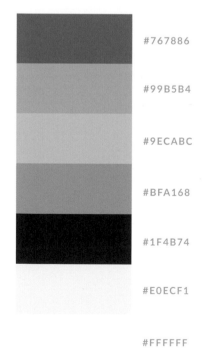

#767886

#99B5B4

#9ECABC

#BFA168

#1F4B74

#E0ECF1

#FFFFFF

TYPEFACES

Playfair Display

Playfair Display Italic

Karla Normal

VALERIE BURGOS
PHOTOGRAPHY

PHOTOGRAPHY IS
the beauty of life captured.

WEDDINGS

ENGAGEMENTS

FINE ART PHOTOGRAPHY
SERVING NEW JERSEY & BEYOND

PORTRAITS

NEWBORN & CHILDR

FAMILY

MATERNITY

MENU

READ *the* BLOG

VALERIE BURGOS
PHOTOGRAPHY

PHOTOGRAPHY IS
the beauty of life captured.

THE VJB EXPERIENCE

WE TREAT OUR
CLIENTS LIKE GOLD.

89

MAKING SENSE OF SEO

with DAVEY & KRISTA JONES

For creative professionals just starting out, can you tell us why Search Engine Optimization (SEO) is important?

Search engine optimization (SEO) is the process of enhancing a website so that search engines (like Google) deliver your content high in the search results to people looking for content like yours. When done effectively, this can increase both the quantity of visitors to your website AND the quality of visitors to your website.

The beauty of focusing on search engine optimization is that there are additional benefits beyond ranking high in relevant search results. You'll become a more effective content creator and marketer in the process, too. And those skills are highly transferable to other platforms (such as Pinterest).

There are primarily three things to focus on when optimizing your website: creating quality content, website structure, and building quality backlinks.

Why is creating high-quality content important, and how do I do it?

It is generally recognized that creating high-quality content that satisfies a searcher's intent is the most important ranking factor. If the content on a webpage is "thin" or low-quality, it's unlikely that page will rank for relevant searches. For example it would be really hard to rank for "Tampa wedding photographer" if your website doesn't have very much content about Tampa or weddings.

There are a few easy ways to make sure you're providing relevant, quality content:

• Do some keyword research to make sure that people are actually searching for the kind of content you want to share. Tools like Ubersuggest are easy and free to use. You'll be able to quickly tell how many people are searching for certain keywords/phrases. You may be considering writing a blog post about the best shoes to wear on a wedding day but if no one is searching for comfortable wedding day shoes, why spend time writing that post? The app will also give you additional keyword ideas (perhaps some with better search volume).

• See what kind of content already ranks for the search. Check out the first page of search results for a given search, and note the similarities between those results. Then make your content better. This might mean making it more thorough and adding additional elements (like video).

• Use tools like Buzzsumo to see what kind of content is being shared across social media platforms. This can also be an effective way for finding similarities between viral content – like types of headlines.

Remember, content doesn't necessarily mean "written content" (although search engines do seem to prefer it). Videos often appear on the first page of search results, too. If you're more comfortable with video, create videos! Consider providing a written transcript, too.

How can I design a website that's user-friendly?

Website structure and user experience are both important because you want people to find relevant content on your website easily and spend more time within your website. When a visitor lands on a website and quickly clicks the "back" button, it indicates to search engines that page may not have high-quality content.

Showit has an awesome collection of free and paid templates to choose from. The advantage of starting with a template is that it was likely created by a professional web designer who had website structure in mind when it was built.

Beyond that, there are things that you can do to make sure that your website is user-friendly:

- Choose colors that look good on the web, and use contrasting colors for links and buttons so that visitors know those elements are clickable.

- Only include the most important pages in the top-level navigation and make sure your navigation can be found easily.

- Tell people where to go next. Include at least one compelling call-to-action on each page.

- Keep things simple and clear. Use Google Analytics to monitor things like bounce rate and time on page, and make adjustments on pages that need it.

- Use a font and font size that can be read easily.

Remember that we now live in a "mobile-first" world—more visitors than ever are using mobile devices to explore websites. It's necessary to have a mobile version of your website that is optimized for mobile traffic.

What's a backlink? And what does that have to do with ranking in the search results?

Imagine you're looking for a restaurant, and you keep hearing over and over again from friends that there's a new taco place in town that you have to try. What are you going to think? You're going to think this new taco place is really, really good.

Search engines use backlinks (links pointing back to your website) to make similar decisions about what webpages are relevant and authoritative. If you write an in-depth post about lighting and a bunch of photographers/bloggers link to that post while writing about lighting, that's an indicator for search engines that your post is authoritative and relevant.

But not all your friends' opinions are weighted equally, right? Maybe a friend who has notoriously poor taste in food recommends a restaurant. You might decide to skip it or save it for later. Likewise, not all backlinks are made equal. Links from authoritative websites like Style Me Pretty or the Knot would be more valuable than a link from a new blog. And links from spammy websites could result in your website being penalized.

How can I use Showit to optimize my website?

The Showit website builder is awesome because you have creative control over your website without having to know any code. This means it's easy to create an optimized website that's user friendly, easy to navigate, and matches your brand without getting "bogged-down" in the technical details.

As I mentioned earlier, give yourself a head-start by starting with a website template

from a designer you trust. Even though the Showit platform is easy-to-use, a professional website designer will build with website structure in mind. This way you don't have to start from scratch and you can rest easy knowing a professional designed your website.

Showit has easy-to-use SEO tools built into the app, too. You can use those tools to add optimized titles and descriptions for every page on your website. Additionally, you also have the option to add the image that you want to appear when a page is shared on social media.

Another aspect of Showit we appreciate is the integration with WordPress for those who want to blog. There are plugins like Yoast SEO that provide user-friendly tools complete with red, yellow, and green indicator lights to let you know whether a page or post is optimized for search engines.

Maybe the most helpful resource, however, is the Showit community. The Showit User Group on Facebook is a great place to ask questions, seek advice, and find support when it comes to SEO or other website and business related topics. And if you want to connect with people in person, you'll definitely want to check out Showit United—an annual conference held in Phoenix, AZ.

This seems like a lot. Where do I start?

Some of these things you have more control over than others. For example, you have complete control over the content you create; however, you have far less control over who links to that content. Focus on the things you have more control over such as content and website design. Doing a good job with those things will often result in everything else falling into place. The important thing is to start.

If you have any questions, you can reach me on our website at daveyandkrista.com or email us at support@daveyandkrista.com.

BEAUTIFUL YOU STUDIOS

🌐 BEAUTIFULYOUSTUDIOS.COM

As a studio for women and by women, visitors might expect to see florals and gold throughout the Beautiful You Studios site. However, much like the experience you will have with the photographer, Candace Perry, this custom site, designed by Andrea Liesting of Sprucestone Handcrafted Digital Design, is an event that exceeds expectations. With Candace's vision and Andrea's web design skills, traditional views of femininity have been forfeited and bold splashes of gold, black and burgundy type have been added for a bold and compelling look. To balance the daring colors, the florals, while present, are of the black, white and gray variety. All of these elements prove that working with Candace will both help web visitors to see their own femininity in a new way, and give women an opportunity to explore what makes them individually bold and beautiful.

DESIGNED BY

ANDREA LIESTING
SPRUCESTONE DESIGN

SPRUCESTONE.CA

COLORS

#000000

#FFFFFF

#2D2B28

#661D16

#E3A8AD

#DFDEDA

#ECEBE8

TYPEFACES

SILVER SOUTH SERIF

Lato Normal

Lato Light

Silver South Script

beautiful YOU
STUDIOS

PERSONAL BRANDING PHOTOGRAPHY

BOUDOIR PHOTOGRAPHY

DALLAS, TEXAS + BEYOND

BEAUTIFUL PORTRAITS
FOR WOMEN, BY WOMEN

Welcome to Beautiful You Studios! We are a for women, by women portrait studio that helps women feel beautiful in both their personal & professional lives through **boudoir photography** & **personal branding photography**. Located in Dallas, Texas, we're available for worldwide travel.

HELLO BEAUTIFUL
I'M CANDACE PERRY,
lover of wildflowers & women power!

READ MORE ABOUT ME

BEST
PHOTOGRAPHER
IN AMERICA

AIR 1 RADIO

TOP 10
PHOTOGRAPHER
IN THE SOUTH

SOUTH MAGAZINE

TOP 25
TEEN PHOTOGRAPHER
IN AMERICA

MODERN TEEN STYLE MAGAZINE

TOP 100
FASHION PHOTOGRAPHER
IN THE WORLD

SOLIS MAGAZINE

beautiful YOU
STUDIOS

PERSONAL BRANDING PHOTOGRAPHY

BOUDOIR PHOTOGRAPHY

DALLAS, TEXAS + BEYOND

THE BEAUTY
OF *boudoir photography*

Boudoir photoshoots are for any woman. If you're comfortable in your own skin, that's amazing! If you aren't however, don't shy away from hiring us to capture your personal beauty. You are beautiful, no matter how many times you may have been told otherwise or how uncomfortable you are being you. Through boudoir photography, my goal is to tastefully capture both the beauty that shines within, & the beauty that others can see when they look at you.

LEARN MORE

THE BOLDNESS
OF *personal branding photography*

If you want to stand out from the competition & bring in the big dollars, a cell phone selfie just won't cut it. Personal brand photography will capture your beauty & brilliance in a professional way. People buy from who they know, like, & trust. If you're online, you must have images that show the personable woman behind your brand in order to build that trust factor. Let me utilize my 15 year background in marketing to create personal

GEORGE & CLAUDIA

🌐 GEORGEANDCLAUDIA.COM

How do you know if your website visitor is your ideal client? Maybe you greet them with a behind the scenes video of you shooting a "madly in love" couple? (Check!) Maybe you work with a designer to create a personal, feminine, editorial vibe that suits a husband and wife team? (Check!) Maybe you ask your web visitor if they are the right couple for you? (Check!) George and Claudia of GeorgeandClaudia.com have a beautiful site that is pretty as well as practical. Working with Ravyn of Three Fifteen Design, they came up with clever ways to make their website work for them. For example, right next to their "Who *We* Are" section, they have a "Who *You* Are" section. Which is just one of the ways they use their online home to help guide visitors to decide if George and Claudia are the right photographers for them.

DESIGNED BY

RAVYN STADICK
THREE FIFTEEN DESIGN

THREEFIFTEENDESIGN.COM

COLORS

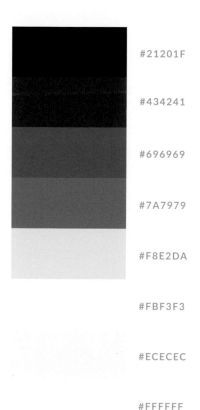

#21201F

#434241

#696969

#7A7979

#F8E2DA

#FBF3F3

#ECECEC

#FFFFFF

TYPEFACES

Montserrat Light

Montserrat Semi Bold

Old Standard TT Italic

Narziss Pro

Alou

naviGatE

GEORGE *and* CLAUDIA

scroll for more

hello, gorgeous

W E ARE GEORGE & CLAUDIA, WEDDING PHOTOGRAPHERS FOR PEOPLE WHO ARE MADLY IN LOVE. OUR WORK TELLS UNIQUE STORIES OF OUR COUPLE'S LIFE, ALL WITH A HIGH-END, PERSONALIZED FEEL. BORN OUT OF A NEED FOR IMAGES THAT FOCUS ON CONNECTION, WE WORK COHESIVELY TO DELIVER IMAGES THAT FEEL AUTHENTIC AND WILL LAST A LIFETIME.

learn more

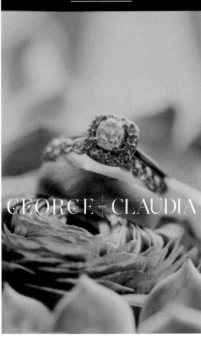

navigatE

GEORGE *and* CLAUDIA

Who We Are

MORE →

ARE WE THE PERFECT FIT?

Who You Are

MORE →

FOLLOW US @GEORGEANDCLAUDIA.CO

INSTA *gram*

EXPLORE OUR FAVORITE HASHTAGS:

#georgeandclaudiacouples

#georgeandclaudiaweddings

navigate

HOME
ABOUT
GALLERIES
THE EXPERIENCE
EDUCATION
CONTACT

read the BLOG

G

PHOTOGRAPHERS for the
MADLY IN LOVE

CONNECTICUT · NEW YORK · CHARLESTON SC
WORLDWIDE

brand & site by three fifteen design
© 2018 george & claudia, wedding photographers

sign up for
the newsletter

f ⃝ 🅿

CLAUDIA@GEORGEANDCLAUDIA.COM

⌃ BACK TO TOP

TANYA & VICTOR

🌐 TANYAANDVICTOR.COM

When you have a website that is inspired by "Restoration Hardware, old letterpress stationery, calligraphy and people who believe in love above all things", you know that you are in store for something beautiful and extremely classic. And that's what Ravyn of Three Fifteen Design created for Tanya and Victor of Tanya & Victor Photography. Their website is not only appealing to the eye but is also so very fun to explore. Their "Meet Us" section will have you clicking and scrolling through a timeline showing the first time the couple ever experienced snow, to the time they eloped! But their website isn't just all fun and good looks: "We have met the most loving of people through our site. Sometimes, it has been a life-changing relationship that started with an inquiry." Tanya and Victor, the talented couple behind the site, are the true joys behind this fabulous design concept.

DESIGNED BY

RAVYN STADICK
THREE FIFTEEN DESIGN

THREEFIFTEENDESIGN.COM

COLORS

#3C3C3C

#5A595C

#ADA9AB

#F2DDD4

#FBEDE7

#FDF7F5

#ECEBE8

#FFFFFF

TYPEFACES

Tigerlily

Pinyon Script Normal

Woolen

Montserrat Normal

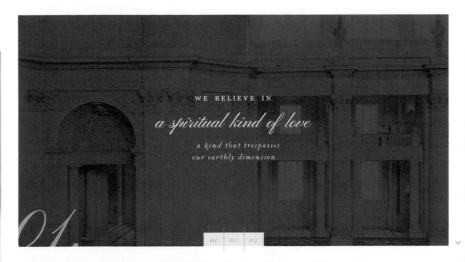

WE BELIEVE IN

a spiritual kind of love

*a kind that trespasses
our earthly dimension*

01. 02. 03.

TANYA & VICTOR

HOME   PHOTOGRAPHS   MEET US   EXPERIENCE   PRESS & PRAISE   INQUIRE   SHOP   *blog*

Navigate

THE EXPERIENCE
IT'S MORE THAN CLICKS
OF A SHUTTER

TANYA & VICTOR
WE FIND OUR TRUEST
SELVES IN THE OTHER

SHARE YOUR HEART
TELL US ABOUT YOUR
LOVE STORY

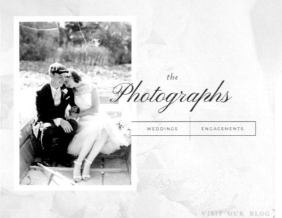

the
Photographs

WEDDINGS | ENGAGEMENTS

VISIT OUR BLOG

HOME   PHOTOGRAPHS   MEET US   *T&V*   EXPERIENCE   INQUIRE   *blog*

CONNECT: ⊙ ⊙ f ⭣ ⭐ ▶

© Tanya & Victor 2018 — Branding by JRS Design

PRIVACY POLICY   TERMS OF USE

01.

WE BELIEVE IN

*a spiritual
kind of love*

*.. a kind that trespasses
our earthly dimension*

01. 02. 03.

2TPHOTO

Thu (pronounced *two*) Tran of 2TPhoto is too fun! And her website and brand are the perfect reflection of that. "I wanted to celebrate the adventurous spirit that my clients and I have. I love the spontaneity created by action and reaction." With initial inspiration provided by the *Hawthorne* design by Three Fifteen Design, this website is jam packed with glorious images celebrating the great outdoors and the free spirits she serves! Whether the hero of the story is getting married at a wedding in Big Sur or some other beautiful and natural environment, love and adventure are at the heart of each of these chosen images. "For a long time I was embarrassed to send people to my site... Now that it's updated with clean lines, and current photos... I have confidence that my work is showcased in a way that makes me proud." And proud you should be, Thu!

DESIGNED WITH
HAWTHORNE BY THREE FIFTEEN DESIGN

COLORS

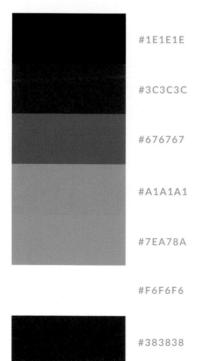

#1E1E1E

#3C3C3C

#676767

#A1A1A1

#7EA78A

#F6F6F6

#383838

#FFFFFF

TYPEFACES

Vidaloka

Cabin

Old Standard TT

Old Standard TT Italic

Raleway Ultra Light

ABOUT ME | THE IMAGES | DETAILS | **2TPHOTO** *Wedding + Portrait* | INVESTMENT | CONNECT | FITNESS

2TPHOTO
Wedding + Portrait

ABOUT ME

HERRO!

MY NAME IS THU--
PRONOUNCED LIKE THE NUMBER 2. I'M A
DESTINATION WEDDING PHOTOGRAPHER BASED
IN ATLANTA.

I LOVE MY FEYONCÉ (♥) ALEK, MY DOG-ELLIE,
IMMATURE JOKES, AND SPONTANEOUS
ADVENTURES. OUTSIDE OF PHOTOGRAPHY AND
TRAVEL, I ENJOY LEARNING. WHETHER I'M
GAINING KNOWLEDGE VIA PODCASTS/AUDIO
BOOKS, OR TRYING BRAZILIAN JIU JITSU, UKELE,
OR YOGA... I'M ALWAYS FILLING MY BRAIN WITH
SOMETHING THAT FUELS MY CURIOSITY.

I LOVE WORKING WITH JOYFUL, LIGHT HEARTED,
AND OPEN MINDED PEOPLE. I VALUE TRUST AND
I APPRECIATE THOSE WHO CHERISH THEIR TIME--
BY DOING WHAT THEY LOVE, BY BEING WITH
THOSE WHO MATTER AND BY ENJOYING THE
BEAUTY, FASCINATION, AND HUMOR IN LIFE.

MY ADVENTURES

ENGAGEMENT

FAMILIES

WEDDINGS

Our Philosophy.

LET'S GET TO KNOW
EACH OTHER!

WE'LL GO ON AN ADVENTURE
AND CREATE A VISUAL TIME CAPSULE THAT REPRESENTS
WHO YOU ARE, HOW YOU FEEL, AND WHAT YOU MEAN TO EACH OTHER.

_____

let's connect!

DAVID MENDOZA III

🌐 DAVIDMENDOZAIII.COM

David Mendoza III is a chronic adventure seeker. The first image on his website is that of a stunning couple, illuminated by rays of sunlight, peeking in through the top of a cave. It is magic personified, which is perfect since he describes his style as "Magical Wedding Photography." With a simple scroll through his online home, even the most skeptical will find themselves believing in his supernatural photography skills. While his site gives automatic proof of his skill, the inspiration for the design came from an unassuming place—his favorite messenger bag. Just as his bag is casually refined, so is his ideal client, as well as his online home. Starting with a template by Tonic Site Shop, David says that his website has given him "a storefront that polishes and creates the perfect expectation for my ideal client." In other words, non-magical people need not apply.

DESIGNED WITH

AMARETTO SOUR BY TONIC SITE SHOP

COLORS

#000000

#F7F7F7

#FFFFFF

TYPEFACES

Didot Regular

Lato Normal

Dear Joe

Lora Normal

Playfair Display Italic

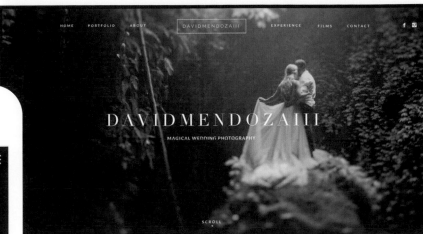

DMIII

DAVIDMENDOZAIII

MAGICAL WEDDING PHOTOGRAPHY

SCROLL

HOME   PORTFOLIO   ABOUT   **DAVIDMENDOZAIII**   EXPERIENCE   FILMS   CONTACT

DAVIDMENDOZAIII

MAGICAL WEDDING PHOTOGRAPHY

SCROLL

Hello, I'm

DAVID

MOST OF MY FRIENDS CALL ME "DOZA"

I'm from a small town on the coast of California nestled between the mountains and the Pacific. I live for spontaneous two-month photo trips to Europe, Mom's enchiladas & chasing after those last little bits of sunlight at the end of the day. I've been in the wedding industry for six years, and behind the camera is where I feel most at home.

READ MORE ▸

THE PORTFOLIO

TAKE A LOOK ▸

A few of my favorite shoots.

FEATURED WORK

KELLCI & CHRIS   **JAMES & JESS**   **EMILY & SETH**   **AUDREY**

TEMECULA, CA   PARIS, FRANCE   PASO ROBLES, CA   PARIS, FRANCE

STORY & RHYTHM

🌐 STORYANDRHYTHM.COM

Tosha and Brian are the husband wife team behind Story and Rhythm Photography & DJ. Combining their skills, they seek to give their ideal clients a wedding experience that goes beyond gorgeous photographs and great music. (Even though, their clients definitely get both!) Going for a clean and classic website, they chose the dapper *Jack Rose* design from Tonic Site Shop. Paired with the images they have selected for their online home—smiling faces, radiant couples, joyous and classy wedding parties, this site embodies their brand and hearts perfectly. Tosha and Brian have found that their website has "strengthened the classic aspect of our business. It also made it easier for us to tie in our brand and to attract our ideal client." Striking the cord between fun and classy, StoryandRhythm.com will have potential clients rearranging their wedding date just to fit in to Tosha and Brian's full calendar!

DESIGNED WITH
JACK ROSE BY TONIC SITE SHOP

COLORS

#040404

#2C3041

#4B5665

#A7A9AB

#A0D4D2

#DFDEDA

#ECEBE8

#FFFFFF

TYPEFACES

Old Standard TT

Libre Baskerville

Amsterdam One

Ubuntu Medium

Timeless, joyful and romantic photographs and epic parties for the modern bride

Hello There!

We're Tosha and Brian and we're a husband and wife Raleigh wedding photographer and DJ team! We believe that marriage is amazing. It is such a special and exhilarating feeling to know that you have found the one who you will spend the rest of your life with. The one who you will walk hand in hand with from now until forever. The one who you can't get enough of. The one who you will build a life with!

We're not your average photographer and DJ! We believe that the best way to ensure an incredible wedding experience is to get to know you as a couple! We take pride in getting to know each one of our couples. We can't wait to help you tell your story!

GET TO KNOW US →

Tips to Help You Plan Your Day

Meet the Team

HOW TO PLAN FOR YOUR
ENGAGEMENT SESSION

3 REASONS TO HIRE A
PROFESSIONAL WEDDING DJ

CREATE A PHOTOGRAPHY
TIMELINE FOR YOUR DAY

FOR BOOKINGS AND
OTHER INQUIRIES   ▸   SEND A NOTE

SWEETLIFE PHOTOGRAPHY

🌐 LOVETHESWEETLIFE.COM

Years ago, Jake and Anna Tenney created a slogan for their brand: "Finely Crafted Love Stories For Joyful Romantics". For them, this is an all-encompassing guide that serves as a filter they run every business decision through. This focus has helped them become known for romantic, joyful, and love-focused imagery with a fine art approach, all of which is clearly depicted on their website. Starting with the *Rendezvous* template, Tonic designer Jeff Shipley customized the design to deliver a website that was "high end, clean, sophisticated", yet still warm and inviting. The Tenneys have been hearing rave reviews about their newly designed site. "Potential clients and industry peers are saying that they feel like they've met us simply by browsing our site, which is leading to easier bookings and bookings that are a better match for us."

DESIGNED WITH
RENDEZVOUS BY TONIC SITE SHOP

DELICATE ACCENTS

0 1

What Makes Us Different

ELEGANT ITALICS

ALL-CAPS WITH
EXTRA KERNING

OUR EXPERIENCE

─────────

TIMELESS SERIF

Like any craft, wedding photography takes time to perfect. We've photographed nearly 150 weddings and we've seen it all (trust us)! Our experience has prepared us to deliver a consistently beautiful result each and every time.

sweetlife
PHOTOGRAPHY

home   meet us   portfolio   offerings   contact   blog

FINELY CRAFTED LOVE STORIES
for joyful romantics

welcome   connect
based in Portland, Oregon
and available worldwide

sweetlife
PHOTOGRAPHY

FINELY CRAFTED
LOVE STORIES
for joyful romantics

PORTLAND, OR

Get To Know

SWEETLIFE

Welcome! We're Portland wedding photographers and a
husband and wife team. Joyful love stories are our specialty.
In fact, we think they have the power to change the world!

MEET JAKE & ANNA

Since 2010 we've been crafting natural, timeless, and
romantic imagery with a fine art approach.

BROWSE THE PORTFOLIO

"THEY CAPTURED SO MUCH HAPPINESS AND
WE'LL FOREVER BE THANKFUL WE CHOSE THEM!"

Lauren & Brandon, Married 7.8.17

01

What Makes Us Different

OUR EXPERIENCE

Like any craft, wedding photography takes time to perfect.
We've photographed nearly 150 weddings and we've seen it
all (trust us)! Our experience has prepared us to deliver a
consistently beautiful result each and every time.

Next   →

ALL THE LATEST ON INSTAGRAM
@sweetlifephoto.jake

home   meet us   portfolio   offerings   contact   blog

AMY & JORDAN

🌐 AMYANDJORDAN.COM

It's hard to tell if Amy and Jordan are better known for being amazing photographers, or incredible educators. When you visit their website, it's obvious they are extremely passionate about both. But how were they able to marry these two different facets of their business on one cohesive site? "Thanks to our brilliant designer, Jen Olmstead, our website is the perfect visual representation of who we are, what we're all about, and what an experience with us is like. It's helped us attract the right clients." For Amy and Jordan, a warm and welcoming online home is their top priority. This is because they LOVE people. At the heart of their photography, as well as their educational outreach, serving people, whether it's a blushing new bride, or a brand new photographer, is felt as much online as it with Amy and Jordan in real life.

DESIGNED BY

JEN OLMSTEAD

TONICSITESHOP.COM

TYPE COMBINATIONS

CONDENSED CAPS

SOPHISTICATED SERIF

BOLD CALL TO ACTION

&

GETTING MARRIED?

Luxury Weddings
for Joyful Brides

LEARN MORE ▶

COLORS

NAVY & BLUSH
A fitting combination to reflect Amy & Jordan

& AMY & JORDAN   HOME   ABOUT   TOOLS   FOR BRIDES   BLOG   STORE   FREE CLASS   LOGIN   **ENROLL NOW**

WE'RE HERE TO HELP YOU

LOVE YOUR PHOTOS
Grow your business
CHANGE YOUR LIFE

Ready to shoot better & edit faster?

ENROLL NOW   **WATCH A FREE CLASS**

Free! PHOTO & BUSINESS COACHING
Delivered straight to your inbox every Monday   **GET YOUR FIRST LESSON NOW ›**

PHOTOGRAPHY TIPS & BUSINESS ADVICE
3 Ways to Learn with Amy & Jordan

WATCH NOW

LEARN MORE

READ NOW

FREE TRAINING

Join us for a free 1-hour class where we'll show you three of our proven techniques you can use to create images you love in-camera.

OUR COURSES

Ready to take your photography or business to the next level? We have three powerful, online, step-by-step courses that will get you there.

FREE TUTORIALS

Learn from us for free! From technical photography tips to practical business advice, click here to get the answers you've been looking for.

FREE I-HOUR CLASS FOR PHOTOGRAPHERS! *Watch Now*

& AMY & JORDAN   ☰

LOVE YOUR PHOTOS
Grow your business
CHANGE YOUR LIFE

Ready to shoot better & edit faster?

ENROLL NOW ›   ⊙ **WATCH A FREE CLASS**

Free! PHOTO & BUSINESS COACHING
Delivered straight to your

MEET YOUR TEACHERS

HEY, WE'RE
AMY & JORDAN

We help people take better photos and build successful photography businesses

LEARN MORE ›

martha stewart weddings   THE HUFFINGTON POST   FOX 10   STYLE ME *Pretty*   BRIDES

"

"While some photographers closely guard their secrets...
Amy and Jordan feel like instant friends who want you to succeed."

- THE HUFFINGTON POST

Student Success Stories

BEFORE & AFTERS

107

JENNA KUTCHER

Scrolling through this site is an exciting journey down a rabbit hole of fun, pretty, education. And it was designed intentionally so. JennaKutcher.com is a wonderful site for all things business, podcast, lifestyle, and photography related. And it was skillfully woven together by Jen Olmstead, who was able to create a cool and relaxed vibe, even though this site is a deep ocean of information and tools for it's website visitors. Jenna has achieved the balance of professionally shot backgrounds and flat lays—showing her skill and style—mixed in with candid shots, and videos of her smiling, and twirling in her chair—showing her joyous personality. Just as with Jenna, those who enter her site are magnetically drawn into this online space and can get lost for hours, learning more about Jenna's business, but more importantly learning more about how to run their own business.

DESIGNED BY

JEN OLMSTEAD

TONICSITESHOP.COM

TYPE COMBINATIONS

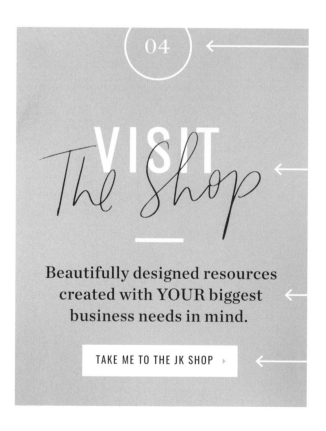

CROPPED ACCENT

LAYERED, JUXTAPOSED TITLE FONTS

HIGH-CONTRAST SERIF

CONTRASTING CALL TO ACTION

photographer, educator, artist

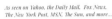

As seen on *Yahoo, the Daily Mail, Fox News, The New York Post, MSN, The Sun,* and more...

Find us through My Curves + Mr. 6 Pack Viral Instagram?

GET THE FULL STORY HERE ▸

ABOUT

hey there!

I'm Jenna Kutcher.

I'm an expert at online marketing, a nerd when it comes to the numbers, and my obsession is teaching others how to make a living doing what they love (without it taking over their *life*).

A small town Minnesota photographer, podcaster, educator and puppy rescuer, my happiest days are spent behind my computer screen sharing my secrets with the world.

LEARN MORE ABOUT ME! ▸

Jenna KUTCHER

MENU

photographer, educator, artist

As seen on *Yahoo, the Daily Mail, Fox News, The New York Post, MSN, The Sun,* and more...

Find us through My Curves + Mr. 6 Pack Viral Instagram?

GET THE FULL STORY HERE ▸

02

WHAT'S *Secret Sauce?* YOUR

How to Own Your Awesome, Stand Out from the Crowd, Build a Successful Biz, and Have Fun Doing It!

CURIOUS? TAKE THE QUIZ ▸

109

HEART'S CONTENT EVENTS & DESIGN

🌐 HEARTSCONTENTEVENTS.COM

"Luxury, heartfelt, marriage-focused" are the first bolded words to stand out on the Heart's Content Events & Design website. Though they are stated after the initial scroll, the visitor will feel it immediately upon arrival to this wedding and event planning site. Adrienne Rolon, the creative behind the business, does not allow you to think that these are the only three words to describe her company. Through a cleverly constructed layout, the designers at With Grace and Gold helped Adrienne share both her heart for event planning and marriage encouragement in a fluid and concise manner. The light blush-toned background alternates with white to allow the visitor to stay captivated by subtle design elements, guiding potential clients from text to image without interruption. The site is so brilliantly designed that the heart of Adrienne Rolon's business will be the first and last impression left on her visitors.

DESIGNED BY

KELLY ZUGAY & ANDRA BARKEY
WITH GRACE & GOLD

WITHGRACEANDGOLD.COM

COLORS

#000000

#191919

#939597

#ECB6BB

#EFE0D2

#F27A9D

#ECEBE8

#FFFFFF

TYPEFACES

Bellefair Normal

Notera

Champagne Bold

Latin Italic

Dorsa Normal

SERVING VIRGINIA, MARYLAND, DC, AND WORLDWIDE

CRAFTING HEARTFELT WEDDINGS SINCE 2014

HEART'S CONTENT EVENTS & DESIGN IS A

LUXURY, HEARTFELT, MARRIAGE-FOCUSED

WEDDING PLANNING AND DESIGN STUDIO
THAT PERFECTS EACH DETAIL FROM BEGINNING TO END
SO YOU CAN FOCUS ON WHAT MATTERS MOST

SERVING VIRGINIA, MARYLAND,
DC, AND WORLDWIDE

∨

HEART'S CONTENT
EVENTS & DESIGN IS A

LUXURY, HEARTFELT

CONGRATULATIONS ON YOUR ENGAGEMENT!
I'M SO GLAD YOU'RE HERE!

I'm your LOVE loving, heart-centered, marriage-focused, peony-obsessed, detail-perfecting wedding planner, florist, designer, and marriage encourager!

I LOVE CELEBRATING MARRIAGE

Throughout this site you'll see heart-wrenching love stories, joyful moments, and reassurance that what I do makes it possible for you to enjoy your engagement, and encourage you through your exciting season of marriage. So go ahead, pop that champagne, and take a journey with me, because

I JUST CAN'T WAIT TO CELEBRATE YOUR
MARRIAGE WITH YOU!

xo,
Adrien

HOW MAY I SERVE YOU?

WEDDING PLANNING AND MARRIAGE ENCOURAGEMENT SERVICES
FOR COUPLES AND CREATIVE ENTREPRENEURS

THE HEART'S CONTENT EXPERIENCE

Love to party? Well, so do I! Here, you'll find out just how we love to serve our couples, so they can sit back, relax, and enjoy their stunning and heartfelt celebration, while I handle the rest.

WE'RE GETTING MARRIED!

MARRIAGE ENCOURAGEMENT

Marriage and business CAN go together like Peanut Butter & Jelly, and here you'll receive

MICHAELA KESSLER PHOTOGRAPHY

🌐 MICHAELAKESSLERPHOTOGRAPHY.COM

If you are about emotion above all other sensations, you will be drawn in to MichaelaKesslerPhotography.com from the get-go. Embodying joy and candid warmth informs the potential client that a photography session with Michaela will in no way be an attempt at posed perfection. "My ideal client is someone who is down to earth, loves to laugh, enjoys a good adventure, and is just real." Michaela, a professional photographer since she was 16, has a fabulous and varied portfolio that will have visitors clicking to her contact page in minutes. After starting with the super-hip *Panama* design by With Grace and Gold, Michaela made it her own to reflect her unique personal brand and connect with the oh-so-lucky clients who will have an authentic adventure in front of this photographer's lens.

DESIGNED WITH
PANAMA BY WITH GRACE & GOLD

COLORS

#333333

#6B6C6E

#D9D9D9

#D5CFC1

#BCC7B7

#FFFAF6

#C3D6C3

#FFFFFF

TYPEFACES

Oswald Light

Montserrat Medium

Belluga

navigate

Michaela Kessler

HOME   ABOUT   WEDDINGS   SENIORS   PHOTOS   JOURNAL   CONTACT

HEY YOU!

I'M MICHAELA, BUT YOU CAN CALL ME MIC.

Erie, PA based photographer and traveling all over. Yearning for going wherever the wind will take me, or at least where my bank account will allow. I believe in good hugs, candid laughter, and road trips!

Read more

Michaela Kessler

01.

SWEET WORDS FROM CLIENTS

"MICHAELA IS SUCH A FUN AND OUTGOING PERSON AND ALWAYS MAKES YOUR SESSION YOUR STYLE!! "

"Never be too shy to ask her anything, she will always help you with poses and even your outfits that you have planned out, just so your session is absolutely perfect! She's so inspirational and will rub that off onto you! "

United

TRANSFORM YOUR PHOTOGRAPHY BUSINESS
IN 4 DAYS

 CONNECT   **GROW**   **STRENGTHEN**

Connect with industry leaders and like-minded creatives in an encouraging and intimate environment.

Gain new perspective and clarity to fall in love with your business all over again.

Strengthen your business and hone your craft through breakout sessions and educational photo shoots.

LEARN MORE
REGISTER → SHOWIT.CO/UNITED

S P A R K

BE THE SOURCE OF INSPIRATION

Get featured in the next issue

APPLY @ SHOWIT.CO/SPARK